Expensive Yanna

I Just Knew

I have four children. While that is a simple reality and an easy thing for me to say, I still recall the first time that I actually spoke those words. It made quite an impression on me, and, I remember it well. It was the Winter of 2007, and I was in my office, talking to a sales rep from a book company. I mentioned children; she asked how many I had, and I responded, four. It was strange to hear the words come from my mouth, almost as if I were listening to someone else speak. But it was my voice, and it was no mistake; suddenly, I had four children, whereas just a few days before I had had only three. What made this so unique, though, was the situation surrounding this fourth child's arrival. Just like her siblings, she was beautiful and perfect, with ten fingers, ten toes, bright eyes, an infectious smile and a loving disposition. But, unlike her siblings, she was nine years old and spoke Russian fluently. And, while the others had come to the world in what Harry Chapin once called "the usual way," this one came to my world on an airplane from a city I had never seen, nearly five thousand miles away.

To understand how this all came about, it is important to understand an experience that may sound familiar to other fathers. Fathers can often seem like the odd-man-out in the whole process of childbirth. We are there at the beginning, of course, main characters in the first act of a lengthy play. But, soon thereafter, we are relegated to a small and supporting role. That is neither good nor bad; it is simply the way things are. We watch as our wives carry our children for months and months. They feel the baby move and grow, and they feel an attachment that we simply cannot easily comprehend. I remember watching my wife interact with our other children before they were even born. She would stroke them and sing to them; she would call them by name. For her that new life was a personal and tangible reality, an individual she could know, and a person to whom she could bond. I would imagine that is true for most mothers. For fathers, though, it is just different; from our perspective our children are little more than an expectation, something that we look forward to and imagine but not yet an actual someone that we can fully know in a real and personal way.

For me at least, that all changed when I saw them for the first time. Moments after their delivery, as I held each one of my biological children, I felt an immediate sense of connection, perhaps similar to the sort of connection my wife had been nurturing throughout her pregnancy. These were my children, bone of my bone and flesh of my flesh, stamped indelibly with my name and identity. They were a gift from the Lord, entrusted to me as a sacred charge and responsibility. For the next two decades at least, and hopefully, for many years thereafter, they would depend on me, look up to me, listen to me and call me Dad. In just being mine, they were different and distinct from all the other children in the world. They would grow up, grow old and eventually have children of their own. Yet, I would always be their father, and nothing could ever change the fact that they would always be my children. It is difficult for me to explain how such a strong connection could develop so quickly, but it did. And because it was so strong and because it formed so immediately, I could actually sense it happening.

Now, I have heard people describe how they experienced a tremendous sense of responsibility when undertaking some significant financial obligation, like closing on a new house or purchasing a business. As they sign the final paperwork, the magnitude of the situation floods them with adrenaline and emotion, and they suddenly feel the weight of the future, with all its many opportunities and risks. Certainly that flood of emotion and expectation has been felt by married couples who, at the moment they exchange their vows and rings, can be moved to tears by the reality of their circumstance and commitment. But, as someone who has done those sorts of things and felt those sorts of emotions, let me assure you that I had never felt quite like this. This sensation or feeling of awareness was simply different. Different in a way that I cannot fully describe but sufficiently different that I can say with some certainty that I had never felt it before and have never felt it again, at least until that one day in December of 2006.

What happened on that particular day? Well, I felt that sensation again when I met my fourth child. Now, as you have certainly reasoned, this fourth child was adopted. But the finalizing of the adoption was really closer to the end of this story than it was to the beginning. Indeed, I knew that this little girl was my daughter long before anyone else knew I was her father. In fact, at the moment of my revelation, she could not speak a word of English and I could not speak a word of Russian. We were just standing there, trying on sunglasses together. We had just eaten lunch and were doing some shopping. Using mostly hand signals, I had told her that she could pick out a pair of sunglasses, having reasoned that she likely did not have a pair of her own. So there we were, just the two of us trying on sunglasses, using the mirror to gauge how we looked and commenting on one another's appearance using a range of gestures and facial expressions.

We were just smiling and laughing when suddenly she looked up at me, through a rather sporty looking pair of shades. She was smiling and laughing, looking for my approval. I could see her eyes, barely, as she stretched forward, tapping on her new lenses so as to draw my focus. In that brief instance, I had that same feeling all over again. Only this time, it took me by complete surprise. This was not a delivery room, and this little girl was no newborn baby. In fact, I had met her for the first time just the day before and this was the first time we had ever spent any real time together. Moreover, we were just standing there by the glasses case and the cash registers, surrounded by complete strangers. And, yet, I felt it again, just as strongly and just as unmistakable as every other time before. While I would not be in a position to talk about this with anyone for quite some time, somehow I just knew and was as sure as I could be at that moment that I had my fourth child.

The Beginning of the Beginning

So, how did we get to that point, and how did I go from sensing something in my heart to actually seeing it come to fruition? Well, it is a long story, involving time and effort, money and travel, frustration and heartache, and lots of bureaucracy and paperwork. In some ways, it was a lot like a pregnancy. All the anticipation and waiting were combined with a healthy dose of preparation and excitement. But this was also very different than a pregnancy. First of all it took longer. From the day I first had that feeling that Yanna was my daughter to the day she actually entered the United States as a legal child of our family and citizen of this country was just over fifteen months. The process was also much less certain. Throughout the fifteen months there was always the chance that some snag in the details would set us back. In fact, the actual adoption process took only about three or four months; the other eleven or twelve months were consumed by bureaucratic foot dragging, paper shuffling and navel gazing. So, even with the guarantee of a favorable outcome, which we never had, we had no way of knowing how long the process would take. And there was always the possibility of an unfavorable outcome. As difficult and as heartbreaking as it may be, it is possible to get right to the end and still receive a negative decision from the court. So, make no mistake of it, adopting a child from the Russian Federation is not for the faint of heart.

The whole thing started in the Summer of 2006. Well, that is not exactly true. Instead, the whole thing really started back in 1975, when the young girl who would later become my wife accepted and turned her heart over to Jesus. As she was filled with the holy spirit of God, she was moved to tears by an overwhelming sense of compassion and sadness for Russia. Why Russia, you ask? Honestly, I have not a clue, and, frankly, neither does she. It is often said, though, that the Lord works in mysterious ways. In fact, the scriptures confirm just that: *"my ways are not your ways and my thoughts are not your thoughts"* is a quote from Isaiah 51. God will often do things that are fully within his will but that to us seem, well, mysterious. Given that, it makes sense sometimes to simply admit that we do not know why things happen as they do. Whatever the reason, though, my wife was flooded with a sense of compassion and longing that moved her, literally, to tears. And she lived with her conviction, with this passion for Russia since she was an early teen. I can still remember her telling me about it when we were dating. She told me then that she planned to marry a man who would work as a missionary in Russia. Of course, she did not know such a man and, frankly, neither did I. I certainly had no intention of being a missionary to Russia or to any place else. Hence, end of story, or so it seemed to me. Far from the end though, that was really the beginning of this story or, to paraphrase Churchill, it was the beginning of the beginning.

What I understand now is that God planted a seed in Cricket's heart. That seed took some twenty years to germinate and thirty years to grow and to bear fruit. But it was a seed nevertheless and, like all seeds, it took time to mature and grow. Looking back now, I can see the process as it developed. Cricket and I were married in 1983 and had our first child, Chase, in 1987, our second, Jaclyn, in 1992 and our third, Christopher, in 1996. Over the course of those years, we would talk periodically about adoption. We agreed that it was a good and humanitarian thing to do, of course. But there were also other things to do as well, houses to buy, moves to make, careers to build and all of that. Like many couples, I suppose, we thought about adoption and about caring for an orphan, but we rarely did much about it. Once we were in our thirties, we actually took some classes, designed to prepare us for hosting foster children. We even identified two biracial children from another state who needed parents and who we considered adopting. But that fell through without us ever meeting them. Also, and to be completely honest about it, Cricket was the one providing most the impetus and motivation to the process during this time. She was the one with the heart for orphans, and she was the one with the sense of imperative and opportunity. I was not opposed so much as I was ambivalent, unsure and inconsistent in my thinking and action. One day I could see myself as an adoptive father, the next I was content with my life and family as it was and saw no reason to undertake a process that was likely to be so time consuming, expensive and difficult. There were simply other things that I wanted and other things that I wanted to do. As many people have likely said to themselves, the timing was just not right. Well, that was the situation that began to change in the Winter of 2006.

The Conversation

Sometime that winter, Cricket had a conversation with Olga. Olga is the wife of an American missionary based in St. Petersburg, Russia. It was a rather complex set of circumstances that brought the two of them together on this day, but the short version of the story goes like this. The missionary is named Mike; he is about my age and grew up in the church we attend, in Athens Georgia. We did not move to Athens until 1996 and, by that time, Mike had moved away. So, we had never really gotten to know him; we had simply heard his name, met him on a few brief occasions and heard about his ministry. After college, he spent several years working and building his career. Along the way, had moved to Texas, and it was there that he was called to minister in Russia. By 2006 he had lived in St. Petersburg for nearly to years and had built a vibrant ministry, serving both the spiritual and physical needs of many Russians, including orphans. I'll say a lot more about orphans in Russia later and the state of the Russian society in the years preceding 2006. For now, though, it's enough to know, that in 2006, there were a lot of orphans in Russia, many of them between the ages of six and sixteen. And, at that age, they are not especially attractive adoptive candidates. First of all, there is not much of a tradition of adoption in Russia. It's just not that common; so few Russian families ever consider it. In the U.S., the situation is different, and adoption is much more common; however, many of the families who are unable to have children in the usual way prefer to adopt infants. Again, that is neither good nor bad; it is just the way things are. However, it can leave older orphans with few options outside of their institutional orphanages. So, much of the work in this ministry that Mike began was for these orphans and the orphanage workers who care for them.

In their conversation, Olga told my wife about a program that brings these sorts of older orphans to the U.S. for short-term visits. These visits are done twice a year at Christmas and in the summer, and they involve children from Russia as well as from other countries like Ukraine and Latvia. The program works like this; you send in a deposit and an initial application. If you are approved at this preliminary stage, you then gain access to a database from which you select the child that you would like to host. After that initial step, you begin a longer process of getting full approval. Once that is done and once the time of the visit arrives, the child you selected is placed in your family for about a month, rather like an exchange program. But it is different from an exchange program in one key way; these children are wards of the state. Your agreement, then, is not with another family but with a foreign government. So, it is a process governed by some very strict rules and by some clear constraints.

During the time the children are actually here, you integrate them into your family's activities, you take them on vacation with you; you show them a good time and allow them to experience life in a loving, Christian family. You also agree to take them to the dentist and the eye doctor (you do not take them to a general physician though - I'll say more later about this too). Finally, when the month is up, you buy them whatever essentials they need, pack up their belongings into a brand new suitcase, pat them on the head lovingly and put them on a plane back to Russia or to whatever country they are from. For them, it's the vacation of a lifetime and it allows them to see a family up close and to feel what that is really like, even if only for a short while. For the host family it is a chance to be charitable and, in a modern day way, to visit orphans in their distress, as the scriptures say. It is rather expensive, $3,000.00 - $4,000.00 in round numbers, and it is time consuming. It requires a substantial emotional investment and requires putting aside many of your normal plans and routines. But it is only a month and, afterward, there is no continuing obligation and no expectation that you will visit or even stay in touch, although many do write and call, for a while at least. Certainly, there is no mention of adoption. Indeed, many of the children are not even adoptable and none of the organizations involved in making this all happen are licensed adoption agencies. Rather, this is simply a loving form of a cultural exchange. It is good for the kids at many levels and has the potential to be a great blessing for the families too.

So, Olga explained this all to Cricket, and Cricket explained it all to me. And, after some talking amongst ourselves and with our other children, some praying, and then some more talking, we decided to say "yes," and to host a child for Christmas. That was August of 2006. Soon thereafter, I contacted New Horizons for Children or NHFC, the organization that handles the American side of the exchange process to express our interest and to get the application packet. I explained to the woman on the other end of the phone, I believe her name was Renee, that we were willing but a bit reluctant. We were not in this to adopt, and we were rather unsure about the sort of child we wanted to host. I suppose you could say that we were picky. The problem was that we really did not know what we wanted. My wife still had a heart for Russia, but I was hoping for a child from Latin America, after all, I spoke more Spanish than Russian, and I had been to Latin America many times, whereas I had never been to Russia. We had no idea what information was available on the children but were simply hoping to "know" the right child when the time came. Upon hearing all of this, Renee gave me access to the database and began talking with me about each child, as I browsed through the pages of pictures and short descriptions.

Each picture was a simple head shot of the child in question. The pictures were taken in the orphanages, where workers from the program had met with, and interviewed each child. Under each picture was a brief description, including the child's age, along with various likes and dislikes. They would go something like this, "Vladimir is 13 years old and in 7th grade. He loves sports, especially

European football, and loves to play outdoors with his friends. He is a good student and speaks a few words of English. He likes most every kind of food but is really fond of McDonald's hamburgers. He has never been hosted before and would like to visit with a family that has a big yard and a dog." Now, I just made that up but it is an example of what you would have to work with in making this decision. After a while, they all began to sound a little bit the same. Moreover, at the time I reviewed the database, there were about 300 such listings, all from kids in Russian or Eastern European orphanages, hoping that someone would spot and pick them to come to America for Christmas.

As I talked with Renee on the phone, I learned that there were no children being hosted from Latin America. Bureaucratic problems had led the program to discontinue its relationship with orphanages in countries like Nicaragua and Honduras and to focus all of its efforts in this particular year on Russia and Latvia. While a bit disappointing, it did not matter much to me. We were simply hosting this child for a month, and it did not much matter where exactly the child was from. I simply scanned each page, looking at the faces and asking questions occasionally about this child or that.

It is funny, now, to look back on that day and on that part of the process. Several of the children that I saw on the database are now well known to me, either because I met them during the hosting program or on subsequent visits to Russia, or because they were later adopted by families that I knew. For example, there was Elena, a young girl who has grown into a delightful and beautiful young lady. She's in college now and I could not be happier for her and for her family. There was Andre, an impressive young man, even at that young age, who now lives with a loving family just a few hours from us. There were Igor, Daniel, Anastasia, Zena and others, all children that I would get to know over the course of the next year. Each one of these and many others had a cute picture and his or her own short story, but none of them felt quite right to me, as I browsed the list. What that really means, I am not fully sure. I did not even know what I was looking for so how could I hope to recognize it when I saw it? But we had prayed about it, and we genuinely believed that God had a plan for this child, even if that plan involved us for only about a month. So, I sat and reviewed the pictures, waiting for the right one to jump out. And, lo and behold, after just a few short minutes, she did just that.

We Want Yanna

Her name was Yanna, and she was 9 years old. She had brown hair, an infectious smile and she seemed excited to be looking back at me. She was wearing a light blue shirt and a necklace of some sort; she also had a clip in her hair. She seemed full of life, like she had just come in off the playground to have her picture taken. She was clearly healthy and happy, with those bright eyes that I mentioned at the beginning. Yet, there was something else; while she was a beautiful little girl, she also seemed somehow vulnerable. She was not undernourished or in anyway unkept. Her story told of how she did well in school, how she liked to draw and sew, and how much she looked forward to visiting America. But there was also something else, something subtle but undeniable that I simply could not resist. It was strange really; I could look at this picture and imagine Yanna running to me and jumping into my arms. I could imagine myself carrying her and tucking her into bed. From the first time I saw that smile, I was just smitten; there is no other way to describe it. And, so, I decided right then that this was to be the child.

So, I asked, what about Yanna? "Oh, she would be a wonderful choice," Renee responded. "She is from Riga, Latvia, has never been hosted and would be a great choice." So, I asked that Yanna be placed on hold, under our name, and I hung up the phone so that I could call my wife.

As I now recall it, Cricket was rather surprised to hear from me. It was still morning and just a day or two after we agreed that we would give this a try and after I said I would call to get the details and the application. I can sometimes be slow in following up on those types of things. Also, I was only calling for details and for an application. Neither Cricket nor I knew or expected that we would select the child so quickly. So, when I called Cricket and told her I had found the child that we would host, she was a bit startled. More than just the timing though, she was startled by my certainty and conviction about our selection, it would be Yanna or it would be no one at all. In essence, we will host if and only if we can host this one particular little girl. Of course, Cricket took one look at the picture and saw everything that I saw. She also noticed that in the description Yanna sounded a lot like our other children. She liked sports, or so the description said, and Chase, our oldest son, was a high school basketball star. She liked singing and performing, or so the description said, and Jaclyn and Christopher were both active in the local community theater and in various plays or choirs at their schools. She liked animals, and we had a dog and a cat. To borrow a phrase, it seemed to be a match made in heaven.

The one issue was that she was not Russian; she was Latvian, and Cricket's heart had always been for Russian children. So, we talked about it and we talked about whether it made any difference. We noted of course that Latvia was a part of the old Soviet Union. Back in the 1970s, when Cricket and I were in high school, for all we knew the Soviet Union was Russia and Russia was the Soviet Union. They were all together, over there somewhere, behind the Iron Curtain, and they all spoke Russian after all. So, we concluded that her calling must have been to the U.S.S.R., which included the people and orphans from Latvia. We also concluded that, at the end of the day, it really did not matter. This little girl was the right child and the right fit for our family; it just felt right to both of us.

And so it was settled; if we were going to host any child at all, we were going to host this one little girl. All that remained was to formalize the selection with a letter to the organization and to lock in the commitment by paying the deposit on the hosting fee. So, I called Renee again and told her that the letter and the check were in transit. She asked if we had discussed our selection and were ready to formally select our child. I simply told her, "yes; we want Yanna."

That was in mid-September of 2006. Yanna would not arrive for her visit until December 14, 2006. In between, there would be paperwork to fill out and a couple of meetings that we would need to attend but not much else. So, this would easy. After all, we were not preparing to adopt, as many families were; we were simply hosting. Still, it was fun and exciting to think about it and to look periodically at Yanna's picture and just to imagine what she was like, what she was doing at the time and what she was expecting. So, I was happy, if a little surprised, to hear from Renee when she called me a week or so later. "Did you receive the packet of application materials," she asked? "Do you anticipate any difficulties meeting the requirements, attending the orientation meeting, or making the payments on schedule, etc.?" "Nope, we are all set and ready to go," I responded. "Okay, well, there is a potential problem," she then said. My heart sank in an instant. I also had an immediate flash of anger. Here we were getting all excited and getting ready to get all the paperwork done. We had reached out to the social worker who would do our home study, to schedule the required visit; we had even contacted all the various agencies that would supply us with all of the necessary documentation. And, now, there is a problem!

I asked flatly, "okay, so what is the problem?" Well, it seems that there were two girls, both named Yanna, that were available for hosting that year and that were on the website. The agency had simply confused the two in their records and, so, in their conversations with me. The little girl that we wanted to host was still available and was still committed to us; however, she was not from Riga, Latvia, as I had been told. Rather, she was from St. Petersburg Russia! Now, as I thought instantly in my mind, how odd that Renee would think this was a problem. After all, what did we care where the girl was from? Cricket had carried around a burden for Russian children for nearly 30 years and, yet, we were willing to accept a child from Latvia. So, did she really think we would back out when we found out that Yanna was from Russia? Given that Renee had never met either of us, I suppose I can forgive her for not seeing the big picture. From our perspectives, though, this was far from a disappointment; this was affirmation! In my mind, I blurted out, "yes!" upon hearing the news. Not only were we doing the right thing by hosting, we had done the right thing by selecting this child! Of course, not wanting to give anything away by seeming too enthusiastic, I quickly ran through all of this in mind before calming myself and responding, "Problem? No, that is fine with us." And, so, it was done; we would be hosting Yanna, a beautiful little girl from St. Petersburg, Russia. I couldn't wait to tell Cricket.

Preparation and Anticipation

As I mentioned we would, we received a thick packet of documents from the hosting service. I still remember taking it out of the envelope and thinking to myself, "Wow, that is a lot of paperwork." Of course, the irony is that this was nothing, truly nothing, compared to what was to come. Still, for a guy who lacks the patience to sign his own credit card slips at the grocery store, this appeared daunting. Part of the problem was that it was all so completely foreign. There was a criminal background check that had to be completed through the office of our local sheriff. I had never done one of those. We needed to have a home study, done by a licensed social worker. I had never done one of those either. There was a lengthy application, asking for all sorts of information about Cricket and me and our children. In addition, we had to submit copies of our drivers' licenses and marriage certificate (finding that was harder than actually submitting it). We had to write statements of faith, explaining how we became Christians and why we chose to host, and provide details on our medical conditions and on the condition of our home. We also had to agree to a fee schedule that had us paying about $2,500, in intervals, over the course of the next few months. Here, too, that sounded like a lot of money at the time. Rest assured the numbers got substantially larger once the adoption process started.

But even if more was to come later, this was still a lot to do, so much so in fact, that it could not really be done privately. When you are taking off work to go the sheriff's office, or spending the afternoon at your desk, filling out an application or writing your personal statement, you are bound to get some questions. So, it was difficult to keep the whole thing secret. Why would I bother trying to keep it a secret?

You know, that is hard to say. Why do couples often keep secret the fact that they are expecting? I suppose it was just a very personal thing. It was something that we had decided to do but I did not want to make a big deal of it. I certainly did not want to deal with a lot of questions about adoption or about why we chose to help a foreign child, when so many in this country need help, too. I simply preferred that we keep the whole thing to ourselves; however, that just was not possible. In fact, the application had to include a letter from my employer, confirming my position and my tenure in it. We also had to have reference letters, confirming that we were good people, who could be trusted to take care of Yanna once she arrived. So, my hopes and intentions aside, this thing was soon to become a public spectacle.

I remember the day the cat came out of the bag at work. I was in my office and had pulled up that picture of Yanna that I had downloaded from the database. My assistant, a woman named Mary, walked in and saw the picture on my computer screen. She knew my children and knew that she didn't recognize this little girl. So, she asked who that was and I explained that it was Yanna, a 9-year old orphan from St. Petersburg that we would be hosting for a month over the Christmas holiday. Upon hearing this, Mary nearly broke down and cried. What a great thing she said. What a beautiful child. What a wonderful opportunity for Yanna, for us and for our other children. It was a real epiphany for me and I almost felt guilty for having tried to keep it all a secret. Here, I had been worried that people would think this whole thing was rather strange or that we were somehow weird for doing it. Yet, Mary was moved to tears at the prospect of this little girl living in an orphanage and of a family half a world away taking her in for Christmas. It may have been out of the ordinary, yes, but far from being weird, it was just what we should have been doing. In fact, I have come to see that this is something that many more people should be doing. Adoption aside, that is truly not for everyone; but hosting is something that virtually every family could and should consider at some point or another. To quote that scripture I mentioned earlier, it is *"pure and undefiled religion"* to visit widows and orphans in their distress. That is what we were doing. So, there was no reason to keep it secret. Indeed, quite the contrary, we were to be announcing it and enlisting the support and prayers of others. And, with only one exception that I recall, all of our friends and family were overwhelmingly positive and supportive.

Interestingly, one of the things that we had to provide as part of our hosting application was a list of potential prayer partners. These were people who would agree to pray for and provide support to us throughout the process. Cricket thought this was great, that NHFC would ask for it and great that we would have this network of partners upon whom we could draw. I have to admit that I was a bit more dubious. What sort of support would we need? What sorts of issues were likely to arise that we could not handle on our own and by ourselves? Heck, why even did we need prayer? Yes, it was fine to pray for Yanna; certainly she needed it. But I was altogether confident that our part was easy and that we were more than up for the challenge. After all, how hard could it be? It is almost amusing to hear myself now and think just how arrogant and naïve I must have sounded. Still, that was really me at the time, at least.

Getting Excited

So, the weeks passed, and we went on about our usual business. Our family spent Thanksgiving in New York, where Christopher was performing in the Macy's Thanksgiving Day parade, as part of a group called Camp Broadway. That was fun. I was working a lot, having recently accepted the position of chair of my department and having tackled a host of new responsibilities. Cricket was readying the house for Yanna but was also kept fully engaged by her responsibilities as wife, mother of three, and director of our household. All the while, though, we were cognizant of our visitor and of her pending arrival. We printed the picture from the database and put it up on our refrigerator. We also had a copy blown up and put it on a poster that we would use to welcome Yanna and to help her identify us when she arrived at the airport. We did some minor redecorating of our guestroom, to make it feel more inviting and comfortable for a 9-year-old girl. I tried to learn some Russian, so that I could at least communicate some basic ideas and help Yanna translate some of her thoughts. That was frustrating, though, because I quickly learned that, without knowing the Russian alphabet, I could not read and learn to pronounce even the simplest Russian words. Cricket made arrangements with some friends who gave us some of their daughter's clothes for Yanna to wear. Remember, she would arrive with virtually nothing. So, we had to provide a wardrobe and necessities sufficient for five weeks. So, we stayed busy with getting ready.

We decided to stay home for Christmas, as was our tradition. The folks at NHFC also recommended this, as it gave the children some stability and time alone and at home with their host families. That sort of family normality, which many of us take for granted, is completely foreign to many of these children and being at home, with a family, for Christmas is exactly what they needed. That made perfect sense, and it was what we were used to anyway.

We did decide to travel to Washington D.C., after Christmas, to visit some family and to give Yanna the chance to see our national capital. We made plans for our "Christmas movie night," which is also a family tradition. We typically go away some short distance for one night right around Christmas, for dinner at some place special and then to a movie or a show. We go into Atlanta mostly but we have also been to Greenville, SC, to Lake Oconee, to Savannah and even to Tampa, FL. With Yanna here, though, we thought that we should do something special and, as it turned out, we had just the opportunity. Cirque du Soleil would be in Atlanta during Yanna's visit; perfect! We searched and found six tickets, on the front row and on the night that we wanted to go. God is good indeed.

By this time, we had also received approval on our home study. We had been given the all clear on our criminal background checks, and we had gotten all of our documents together and sent in. As a part of our package, we wrote a letter to the director of Yanna's orphanage, requesting that Yanna be allowed to come and stay with us for Christmas. In that letter, we promised to care for her and to provide for her safety and health during her visit. We even wrote a letter to Yanna. This was also required, but it was far from perfunctory. This was our opportunity to make Yanna feel welcome and safe. Remember, I said that, in her picture, she somehow looked vulnerable. Well, we wanted her to know she had nothing to fear. We were nice people, with a cat and a dog and children of our own who were about her age. We were looking forward to her visit and planning some fun things. We wanted her to be excited and to look forward to meeting us, just as we were looking forward to meeting her. So, we put all that in the letter. Of course, none of the orphans, Yanna included, spoke English so the NHFC staff had our materials translated before sending them to Russia and to the appropriate offices and orphanages. A copy of the letter we wrote to Yanna is below.

Dear Yanna,

Hello! We are excited you are coming to visit us and we hope you are excited too. To help you get to know us, we wanted to write and say hello.

To begin, we are Allen and Cricket Amason. We are both 44 years old and we have been married for 23 years. We have 3 children; Chase is 19 and a university student. Jaclyn is 14 and is in 9th grade. Christopher is 10 and he is in 5th grade. We have a dog named 'Grits' and a cat named 'Daisy' and we live in Watkinsville, Georgia in the USA. Watkinsville is a small town, about an hour from Atlanta.

We live in a house, in a neighborhood with lots of children. Christopher and Jaclyn both spend a lot of time outside with their friends, when they are not in school. They go to school at 8:00 in the morning and come home around 3:00 in the afternoon. During school, Chase lives at his University which is about 2 hours away. At Christmas though, they will be on holiday. So you will be able to see a lot of them and we will be able to do a lot of things together.

We were able to read a little about you and we learned that you like many of the same things we like. We read that you like basketball. Well, Chase, Jaclyn and Christopher all like basketball too and all play basketball for their schools. If any of them has a game while you are here, we will take you so that you can watch. We also read that you like singing. That is great because Jaclyn and Christopher both like singing too. In fact, both Jaclyn and Christopher are in a play right now and both of them sing and dance on stage. If there is a play in town during your visit, we will try to go together to watch it. We will probably go into Atlanta too. Each year around Christmas, we like to go into Atlanta for a day; we do some shopping, have dinner at a fun restaurant, and go to see a movie. It is a lot of fun and we think you will enjoy it.

Most days though we do the normal things that many other people do. The kids go to school, Allen goes to work as a university professor, and Cricket works around the house. In the afternoons or on the weekends, everyone is home. The kids do their homework and then play with their friends. We have supper together; we watch some television and then we go to bed. Our house has an extra bedroom, for special guests. The room is pink, with a window that looks out on the street. That is where you will stay. Even though it will all be different and new, you should find it very easy and comfortable. You will also find that it is much warmer here than in Russia! In fact, we rarely get snow. Last year, we went all winter and it did not snow at all.

So, we look forward to seeing you and we want you to have a wonderful time while you are here! We hope you are well and we will think about you often until you arrive.

Sincerely,

Allen & Cricket Amason

We had also enlisted the support of our prayer partners. As an aside, let me tell you briefly about these people. They were nothing short of intercessors, standing in the gap for us and for Yanna. They bore the burden of our commitment during all the struggles that would come, but they took none of the credit. They prayed for us; they offered to help us with the logistics. One of them even gave us a check for $200.00. By the way, I can't tell you how touched I was by this. All that we have ever needed, God has provided. We have never really struggled or suffered, and we have enjoyed many things that others have not. And yet, here were these friends giving us money, simply because they did not want us to bear the burden alone. God bless them. It was a very exciting time. Christmas was coming, and that is always a special thing. But this year in particular would be different and exceptional, and we could feel the excitement and the energy.

At least that was true of Cricket and me. Cricket could, of course, feel one of her life's dreams coming to fruition. While we had agreed with one another that this was no precursor to adoption and that we were doing this just as a temporary hosting, Cricket could still sense that, somehow, she was finally making progress toward that calling God had placed in her heart many years before. As I said, though, we agreed that this was not a first step towards adoption, and I believe that she genuinely meant that when we agreed to it. To this day, we still joke about going for a test drive and then falling in love the new car. But it really wasn't like that. We were very clear about it; we were happy to be hosting, but that was all. In fact, during our orientation meeting with the hosting agency, we introduced ourselves as such and heard the NHFC director, a woman named LeAnn, explain how this attitude was healthy and appropriate. It was not fair to the child or to the family to consider this a trial run or an audition. Moreover, adoption or no, it was a tremendous opportunity for each one of us to love a child in a way that child had likely never been loved before and to bless that child with an experience of a lifetime and a memory that could very well change the trajectory of her future. That alone was enough, and that by itself was exciting.

Our children, though, were probably a bit less excited, on the whole. I don't suppose that is too surprising. They were, after all, pretty young and pretty well caught up in their own activities. Still, they would join us in the excitement at times, joking for instance that we would arrive at the airport expecting to see little, 9-year-old Yanna, and finding instead 17-year old Igor. The joke went something like this; the hosting agency used the pictures of cute, smiling kids as a ruse. They would then bait-and-switch the gullible families with hard drinking, hard smoking, behavioral problems from the orphanages. The orphanages paid the agency to run the charade as a way of getting these fictitious, troubled kids out of the country and getting the orphanage workers at least a month of peace and quiet. As we joked about it, it was rather like a Little Orphan Annie meets the Mariel boatlift story and the kids loved embellishing it. I have to admit that it was funny, given that it was so highly unlikely, of course.

But there were times as well that small bursts of resentment surfaced. This was especially true in the case of our daughter, Jaclyn. I'm not sure whether she was anticipating a future that even I had not yet anticipated. Or, maybe, she just did not want to share the spotlight as the only beautiful little girl in the family, even if she was sharing it only for a few brief weeks. The boys, too, though would occasionally express some frustration with how all of our plans revolved around Yanna and her visit. I suppose I can understand their hesitations; they were just kids, too, after all. By and large though, those instances were few and far between. Overall and on balance, I think the kids were pretty excited, too. This was something new and something different, and they could sense and were infected by our excitement. It was an adventure, and, temporary disagreements and inconveniences aside, an adventure that we were taking together.

The Day Arrives

Yanna arrived on December 12, 2006; it was a Tuesday and I remember it like it was yesterday. By chance, it was also the day of my department's annual Christmas party. That actually turned out to be a good thing. I was going to need to leave early, in order to be at the airport on time. The whole family was going; we were going to leave as soon as the kids were out of school, which meant that I would leave the office about 2:30, and we would all get in the car and try to leave the house around 3:30, in order to be waiting in the lobby of the Atlanta airport by 5:00. Beyond just that, though, I suppose I was relatively worthless in terms of work. I was genuinely excited and completely distracted; Cricket was practically giddy and called me no less than once an hour to talk about this, that or the other thing. All of our friends knew about it and the folks at church were abuzz. So, it was a fun day and one where it was hard to maintain focus. It was also one day after I began my informal e-newsletter.

This newsletter circulated through email and began as a simple means of communicating with our prayer partners and friends. We were supposed to keep people informed and to solicit their prayers and this seemed an efficient way to do that. Over the weeks and months that would follow, though, the newsletter would grow to be much more than just that. I believe the first one was sent to only about 10 or 12 families and individuals. These were our closest friends along with that small group we had enlisted to pray for and help us during the hosting period. By the time I sent the final letter, it was going out to between 70 – 80 families and individuals, and many of those were forwarding it on to many others. So, it was reaching a lot of people. Over this same time it became a therapeutic exercise for me, a way to express what I was feeling in writing, without having to repeat it over and again each time I was asked and without risking being overwhelmed by emotion. It was also a way to document the experience. While the memories still linger in my mind, it is nice now to be able to look back and to read those emails. Like looking through a yearbook or listening to the oldies on the radio, they simply call to mind all that was going at the time and all that I was feeling on that day. I can close my eyes and put myself back in each moment and remember it as it was. So, for a host of reasons, I am glad that I did it, and I am glad to have kept all those notes and to be able to recount them. I have copied the first installment:

December 11, 2006

Thank you for agreeing to pray for Yanna. She will leave St. Petersburg this evening, likely around 4:00 p.m. our time. In St. Petersburg, that will be about midnight. She will have a long train ride and then a long flight to Atlanta. Counting the wait times and time needed to clear customs and immigration, it should take nearly 26 hours, from the time she leaves until she meets us in the airport. So, please begin praying today. Pray that her departure will go smoothly and that her travel will be safe. Pray also that she will be able to sleep along the way, that she will not get ill, and that she will be excited and looking forward to her arrival.

We are excited and looking forward to tomorrow afternoon. If all goes well and with the trip back to Watkinsville, we hope to have her home by 9:00 Tuesday night. By that time, it will be 5:00 a.m. Wednesday morning in St. Petersburg. So, Tuesday will be a long day for that little girl.

Blessings,

Allen

It was a simple little message, sent the day that Yanna left St. Petersburg. In many ways, it was the first step in a very long journey, for all of us. It was a trip that changed our lives. And, as I expected, it did take about 26 hours. Yanna left the orphanage and traveled by bus to the Moscow train station in downtown St. Petersburg. From there, she and the other children boarded a train that would take them, overnight, to the Leningrad station in Moscow. There they were met by a bus that took them on the long ride from the train station to the Sheremeteyvo airport, where they boarded a plane for the 12-hour flight to Atlanta. From there, it would be another 2 – 3 hours or so before she was resting, in our house. So, for her, it was in fact a very long day.

For us though, the day seemed to take almost as long, as the time crept along at the pace of a glacier. Throughout my day, I would pull up the Delta website and track Yanna's flight. I had just discovered this neat functionality that would allow me to actually track the flight. Much like the in-flight tracking graphic that you will see on a plane, the website displayed an image of a plane, superimposed on a Google Earth-styled map. You could click on the plane and get a display of the location, altitude, speed, distance from origin and estimated time of arrival. Like a kid with a new toy, I was transfixed. So, while my colleagues enjoyed our departmental party, I ducked into my office every five to ten minutes to update the progress. And I would ask myself silently, what was Yanna doing on that plane? Had she studied and learned enough geography to understand where she was and how close she was getting? As she got over land did she realize that she was over the United States and did that mean anything to her? Was she thinking about us, perhaps looking at the pictures or reading the letter than we had sent her? In all likelihood, she was doing none of this. Rather, she was likely watching the on-board entertainment system, passing the time sleeping or talking to her friends, or simply enjoying the free snacks and drinks. After all, she was nine years old and in most respects, no different from any other nine year old. Still, it was fun to think about.

At about 1:30 that afternoon, I left to come home. At that time, the flight was somewhere over Ohio, headed south for Atlanta. Because the flight originated in Moscow, which is far north of Atlanta, the plane followed a path that took it up, over Iceland and Greenland, across northeastern Canada, and then almost due south to Atlanta. So, by early afternoon our time, they had crossed the Atlantic Ocean and Canada and were now in U.S. airspace. Our house is about an hour and a half from the Atlanta airport, and we did not want to be late. So, I came home around 2:00, to find that Chase, who was home from college, had washed and cleaned the family minivan. So, sometime between 2:30 and 3:00 we left the house, stopped to pick up the other two kids from school, and headed to the airport, ahead of schedule.

Along the way we retold some of our jokes about the whole process. Perhaps, we would show up to find a 17-year named Igor, with a taste for cigarettes and beer, and a lengthy criminal record. Or, maybe Yanna was actually a spy, a young but accomplished agent of the KGB, now the FSB, who, despite her innocent appearance, was, in fact, a master in the ways of espionage. Our young guest would set up in our house an electronic surveillance system beyond anything seen in a James Bond movie. Of course, none of this was true in the least; still, it was fun to laugh about. We did wonder seriously, though, what would happen if Yanna hated us, along with the whole process of hosting? What if she had been sent here against her wishes and resented everything about the experience? She would be here for five weeks after all. Certainly, the time would pass quickly if the fit was good. But if the fit was not good; well, no one really wanted to think about that.

By the time we parked the car, it was nearing 5:00, and the children were supposed to be in the lobby of the airport by 5:30. So, we hustled in and found the spot. To those who are not familiar with it, the Atlanta airport is the busiest in the world. In the weeks before Christmas, volume can easily reach 300,000 people per day. And, on this particular day, it seemed that every one of them was trying to stand in precisely the same spot. We were to meet the children at the top of a long escalator, where everyone who disembarks in Atlanta enters the main terminal from the flight gates. It is a crowded area anyway but on this day it was especially so. You see, while most people wait there for just a few minutes, until their party arrives and then they leave, we were part of a large group and we were all there for over an hour. Our efforts at punctuality aside, getting 60 or so Russian and Latvian minors and chaperones, few if any of whom spoke English, through the immigration, customs and security desks at the world's busiest airport took a bit longer than anticipated. You have to remember, too, that these were children, few if any of whom had ever seen the inside of an airport, ridden on a plane or been to a foreign country. Rest assured that the scenery was different from anything that they had ever experienced. And, so, it all just took some time.

Back at the top of the escalator, the families just stood and waited. Most had made posters, like ours, with a picture and the name of the child. Some had even gone so far as to write, in Russian, the child's name or things like "welcome" on their posters. Show-offs. Many people had balloons or stuffed animals as welcome gifts and most everyone had a camera. It became a point of social comparison for the children and me. We looked at each family and wondered how much work they had put into the preparation. Perhaps they had done this before; maybe someone in their family spoke Russian. Some looked happy and excited and others not so much. Comparing ourselves to others is simple human nature, I suppose, and we embraced it to the fullest as a way to pass the time.

Speaking of cameras, one of the local television stations sent a crew to cover the arrival. It was news after all and the hosting organization wanted to publicize the work. So, the station had sent a reporter and camera crew. And, naturally, they all set up shop right in front of me. I remember thinking, "nice, I get here early, pick out a good spot where I will have an unobstructed view of the escalator and these knuckle-heads come in at the last minute and park themselves right in front of me!" So, I introduced myself to the reporter and the cameraman and told them of my plan; at the moment the children come up the escalator, I was going to jump in front of the camera. Consequently, the viewers of the evening news that night would see nothing more than the back of my head. The reporter seemed a bit irritated at this; however, he quickly discerned that I was completely serious. So they found another spot. Meanwhile, my own children threatened to leave me because of their embarrassment.

Finally, at about 6:30, after more than an hour of waiting, the phrase "here they come" began rippling through the crowd. Everyone strained forward, shoulder to shoulder pushing ourselves into a tight semi-circle into which the children would fall as they stepped off the escalator. I do not really recall who came up first; there was just a mass of children and noise, followed by a confusing few seconds of families identifying their children and pulling them out of the crowd. Because of the crowds, I held up the poster and began calling Yanna's name. I had been looking at her picture for nearly three months, so I knew what she looked like. But try as I might, I just could not find her amidst the chaos. In fact, I was getting a little frustrated when my children behind me said, "Dad, she's right here." Looking down, I saw a little girl, standing right in front of me, but just below the angle of my gaze and just under the poster that I was holding up. I suppose, at that moment, I felt a little silly.

As I mentioned, I had studied that picture from the database for weeks, months even. So, I knew what Yanna looked like, and I knew what to expect. But that was just the problem; the little girl that I was expecting was not quite the person standing in front of me. She was shorter, with darker hair, and a heavy winter jacket, with a thick collar that was zipped up to just below her nose. And she certainly was not smiling. In fact, to say that she was not smiling does not begin to do justice to her expression. This was a look of active of displeasure. If this was, indeed, Yanna standing in front of me, then she was not happy to be there.

So, I knelt down and using, or abusing, what little Russian I thought I had learned, I said hello and introduced myself. I put my arm around her shoulder and tried to introduce the rest of the family. She was not interested and simply stared straight ahead. Oh boy, I thought this is going to be a fun visit. Ironically, we have since learned that she did not recognize us either. We had sent her pictures of our family, along with that introductory letter that I mentioned earlier. For one reason or another, though, apparently we did not look in real life like we did in the pictures. Christopher had died his hair as part of his costuming for a play at the local community theater. Jaclyn had hurt her ankle in a basketball game at school and was on crutches. We were all a bit less polished than we were in the photograph, and we were tired from the long wait, so we just did not look like the people in the picture, and Yanna was a bit confused. She also had a slight fever and was bit pale, perhaps from the travel and the lack of sleep. So, we all just stood there, awkwardly.

Soon enough LeAnn, the director of NHFC came over. With her was a middle-aged Russian woman, named Lydia. Lydia was the director of Yanna's orphanage and a strong supporter of the hosting program. Lydia was also a no-nonsense woman, whose position carried considerable responsibility and prestige. Unfortunately, Lydia spoke no English. LeAnn however, spoke a little Russian and there were also translators, paid by NHFC, who were there helping to sort out everyone and everything. LeAnn introduced us to Lydia and confirmed to us that this was indeed our Yanna. Through the interpreter, we were able to find out that Yanna was not likely sick but, perhaps, just tired. She had also received a bump on the nose, causing a slight nose-bleed, while on the underground transport at the Atlanta airport. Lydia appeared to scold Yanna mildly for being so standoffish and then she reassured Yanna that we were the family to which she was assigned and that we were nice and trustworthy people. We then had a group picture taken, Yanna, Lydia and our family. The photograph was a requirement of the Russian government; it was sent that very night to the Russian authorities, to confirm that the children had arrived safely and had been handed off to the proper families by their chaperones.

With the picture taken, we were free to leave. Yanna had brought with her only that heavy winter jacket, a backpack and a small paper bag. The bag was rather like a gift bag or a shopping bag, with colored paper and looping handles. She clutched it tightly and would not let anyone touch it. She did though agree to let Chase carry her backpack as we walked out of the airport together. I remember getting to the car and asking Yanna if she wanted to take off that hot and heavy jacket. The answer was an unambiguous 'nyet.' She climbed into the minivan and chose the single seat behind the driver; Cricket got into the seat beside her. Again, Cricket asked if she wanted to take off her jacket; again the answer was 'nyet.' Remember my comment about this being a long five weeks? Well, no sooner had I started the engine than the jokes and comments began. "What have we gotten ourselves into?" "Remind me again why we decided to do this?" "Well, this is sure going to be a fun five weeks!" We were all confident that Yanna could not understand a word we were saying, so we laughed at each comment and so encouraged one another to continue. And so you can imagine our surprise when, in the middle of this, Yanna blurted out, in crystal clear English, "I need to go to the bathroom."

Of course, she probably did have to go. But that was completely beside the point. She had just spoken to us and spoken to us in English, with crystal clarity and with no hint of an accent! We immediately began to quiz her; did she understand us? Could she speak English? What else did she have to say? She issued back a steady dose of dead silence. So, we stopped at a gas station where Cricket took her to the bathroom. Once inside the building, it turned out that she did not need to go after all. To quote Alice, this was getting curiouser and curiouser. So, we got back in the car and continued home. Upon getting back into the van though, she chose to sit in the back, next to Jaclyn. As we drove, she began to hold Jaclyn's hand and to relax. Ultimately, she fell sound asleep.

Russian Orphans

Russia is the largest and most powerful of the 15 republics that once made up the Union of Soviet Socialist Republics, often referred to simply as the Soviet Union and abbreviated as the U.S.S.R. The U.S.S.R. was created in 1922 and was one of the allied powers, aligned against Nazi Germany in the 2nd World War. It was also the chief sponsor of expansive communism throughout eastern Europe, Asia and Central America after the war. For the 40 or so years, from the late 1940s through the 1980s, the U.S.S.R. was the rival superpower to the United States and a secretive and closed country to most of the free world. Because Russia was so dominant in this federation of quasi-distinct, subnational states, the whole of the Soviet Union was often referred to simply as Russia. The capital of the U.S.S.R. was Moscow, the capital of Russia. The official language of the U.S.S.R. was Russian. Most of the various symbols of the Soviet Union, such as the familiar red star, were formerly symbols of Russian nationalism. Moreover, the early events that led to the birth of the Soviet Union, such as the "Bloody Sunday" massacre of protestors in 1905 and the October Revolution, where the Bolsheviks initially came to power, occurred in Russia. It is no surprise then that, for much of the world, the two countries, Russia and the U.S.S.R. were seen as being one in the same. Even Winston Churchill, who in 1939 described Russia as "a riddle wrapped in a mystery, inside an enigma" was actually referring to the U.S.S.R. and not just the Russian republic.

But all of that changed in December 1991. Following a long and slow decline, the Soviet Union ultimately broke apart, and the Russian Federation assumed all of the obligations of the old union. While the various benefits and costs of this break up will be debated for generations, some things about it were clear almost from the start. The first is that it unleashed a wave of social and economic turbulence so great that there were few historical precedents. The U.S.S.R. was a superpower with a population in 1990 of more than 290 million. It was a country with little or no tradition of individualism or self-determination, as the communist government had been preceded by the tsars and by centuries of autocratic rule. It was a culture of fierce pride and resilience, though, given the suffering and the ultimate victory that had been won there during World War II. In fact, most Russians see the Soviet Union as the "winner" of the 2nd World War, albeit with some moderate assistance from the British and the Americans. They were also the first in space, with Sputnik being the first satellite to achieve a sustainable earth orbit, Yuri Gagarin was the first "cosmonaut" or human to reach outer space and Valentina Tereshkova was the first woman in space. The U.S.S.R. had a strong athletic system, and for years had been the dominant country in both the winter and summer Olympics. The U.S.S.R. even hosted the summer Olympics in 1980, the year that the U.S. boycotted in protest of the U.S.S.R.'s invasion of Afghanistan. Of course, Russian ballet, literature and music were revered around the world. So, they were a people proud of their country and its accomplishments, but, also, a people with little or no knowledge of or experience in international affairs, free market economics, democratic processes or self-governance. Moreover, as a people, they had little real understanding of international finance or of how impoverished their country really was.

The reasons for the poverty are nearly as complex as the reasons for the collapse itself. Put simply, the U.S.S.R.'s economy did not produce much that was of value to the world market. Moreover, its currency, the Ruble, was not traded internationally and had no value outside of the country. The principal exports were oil and gas and selling these commodities was one of the few ways the country could raise hard currency. Internally, the economy was centrally planned, slow and inefficient. Lacking market incentives, there was little innovation, little attention to quality and gross underutilization of talent and resources. So, the country depended on imports for many things but most of all, for its food. Unfortunately, though, the large Soviet military and the expansive foreign policy consumed much of the hard currency that could have otherwise been spent on food, infrastructure and social welfare. So, the people of the Soviet Union suffered frequent hardships and shortages. Moreover, the lack of innovation and quality eventually began to impact even the production and export of oil and gas, exacerbating the hardships and shortages all the more. Thus, when the Soviet Union collapsed, the country was essentially broke with far more liabilities than assets and little in the way of resources or capabilities that could quickly be adapted to market realities.

Sheltered as they were, though, the people of Russia knew little of this and so were ill-prepared for the calamity that followed December of 1991. Within two years the Russian Federation, lacking hard currency or tradable assets, was forced to default on the debts that it had assumed. This led to a dramatic decline in the value of the Ruble, effectively wiping out savings and retirement accounts and leaving even those who had once had money unable to buy the basic necessities of life. With no customers, the fledging private businesses that had sprung up quickly failed; thousands upon thousands of workers were suddenly unemployed, and the economy just ground to a halt. In the face of such desperate and chaotic circumstances, crime and drug use escalated, corruption and the black market thrived and people began to question and doubt many of the basic institutions that had long been the foundations of their society. Like having the rug pulled out from under you, many Russians found themselves suddenly without any firm sense of security or certainty. Their jobs were gone; there was no money and there were few if any goods to buy anyway. With virtually no warning, their world had simply collapsed around them, and they were left with little or nothing to hold on to. And, so, their frustration turned to depression and their depression turned to despair.

It was this generation of despair that gave birth to the millions of children who were housed in Russian orphanages in 2006. Many of these children came from good families who were simply torn apart by the social and economic upheaval that overwhelmed Russia in the 1990s. While every situation was different, there were common themes across many of the stories. A young couple would marry in the late 1980s or early 1990s. They would begin a life together and have children; however, the events of the early and mid-1990s would take their toll. The couple would often fall into poverty and then into alcoholism, followed often by crime, prison or worse. The children would be neglected or even abandoned altogether. Sometimes, grandparents would step in to help, but they were often limited and unable to assume full control. So, the children would be taken by the authorities and placed into state orphanages. Other times, a young woman would lose her job and be unable to find work. She might sell her apartment and move in with a boyfriend or husband, only to be subsequently abandoned and so find herself with no place to live. With no money or housing, she would turn to drugs and to prostitution as a way to survive and to support her addiction. As a prostitute and a drug user, she would be deemed unfit to care for her children and they would be taken away upon their birth and, again, placed in an orphanage. Still another theme had parents breaking down under the stress of their circumstances and losing touch with reality. These otherwise loving parents lacked the mental and emotional capability to deal with their children and to care for themselves. Many were then institutionalized and their children, again, placed into state orphanages.

It was a sad reality of circumstances that swept over the country, disrupting the anticipated paths of individual lives, undermining confidence in the traditional values of education, work and family and tearing apart the social fabric that had supported the secure life the Russian people had once known. Some coped, adapted and, ultimately, got by, but others simply stumbled and fell, never to get back up. And, amidst the wreckage of this enormous society were millions of children, some of whom were on the street but many of whom were placed in orphanages, where they could at least be fed, housed and schooled but where warmth, hope and love were otherwise in short supply.

This was the world into which my daughter, Yanna was born. To protect her privacy, I will not tell the whole story of how she ended up at an orphanage. Some stories are best left untold. She did come from a family that was once full of potential and promise, and I fully believe that, for a time at least, her parents truly loved one another and this little girl that they had named Yanna. But, like so many others, they were knocked violently off the track that led to a healthy and productive future. They fell into unemployment and alcoholism; the father began to associate with a rough and likely criminal crowd. The mother struggled to hold her family together but could not control the forces that tugged on and tempted her sons and that, ultimately, took the life of her husband. In utter despair, she lost her will and was consumed by her addictions. Yanna was moved to various foster homes and then into an orphanage. Because she was so bright and because her limited family experiences had provided her with relatively good social skills, she was soon transferred to an orphanage for especially talented children. This orphanage was directed by Lydia, the wise and loving woman who we met at the airport. The home was also connected to a good school and had an academic supervisor who was demanding but who also had the best interests of children at heart. Finally, it was an orphanage where 60 or so other bright and engaging children lived. So, while it was no family, it was still a good place where Yanna was safe and warm, well-fed and well-protected. And, because it was a good place, it was the perfect place for NHFC to visit and to find children with great potential, who could benefit from the hosting process and who could offer the sort of enthusiasm and promise that would attract the attention of a family such as ours.

We Are All Smitten

It was about an hour after Yanna fell asleep in the backseat of our minivan that we pulled into our neighborhood. As we made that last turn she somehow knew it was time to wake up. She did so without saying a word; she just sat up and began looking out the windows, at all of the Christmas lights arrayed on the houses and lawns on our street. It was a crystal clear and cold, almost early winter night, and the lights filled the street with color and energy. After a moment or two, Yanna exclaimed quietly, "ooooh..." It was really her first expression of pleasure since our initial meeting, and we all sensed that her mood was changing.

We pulled into the garage and began to unload. In my very rudimentary Russian, I said to Yanna, "this is our house." She nodded in understanding. We opened the door and Grits, our miniature cocker spaniel was there to greet us, barking loudly and sprinting around in circles. Yanna was delighted. We took her inside where she met Daisy, our cat. Daisy was from an orphanage of sorts, too. We had gotten her earlier in that same year from the humane society animal shelter and had selected her for no reason other than that her gray color reminded us of the previous family cat. Interestingly, though, Daisy was later found to be a Russian Blue Point. So, Yanna took to her almost instantly. Kawska is the Russian word for cat and Yanna said it over and over as she chased Daisy through the kitchen. Daisy was completely traumatized by the experience and disappeared for days. Yanna, on the other hand, was beginning to open up and beginning to realize that her adventure was turning for the good.

We seized the opportunity and immediately began taking her around the house, showing her the kitchen, the bedrooms, the den and playroom. Having known only the small apartments common in Russia, as well as the orphanages in which she had lived, Yanna marveled at the size of the place and at the way it was decorated for Christmas. In particular, she was fascinated and amused by the footswitch that turned on and off the Christmas tree lights. I showed her how to use it, and she must have hit that button a dozen times. Somewhere along the way, at some point during the tour, Yanna took my hand. Or perhaps she let me take hers. Truthfully, I don't remember just how it happened. I just recall that, by the time we walked into our guestroom, the room that would become hers, she was holding my hand. "This is your bedroom," I told her, again in broken and bad Russian. She stood for a moment and looked around. Then she climbed up on and sat on the bed. She looked around smiling as all of us spilled into the room, forming a semi-circle around her.

Chase, was still carrying the backpack that she had brought with her from Russia. She asked to have it and he obliged. She slid around to the side, opened her backpack and began to unpack and display its treasures. The first thing she took out was the letter that we had sent her. It was now translated into Russian but was otherwise identical to the original. It was still decorated with various cartoon characters, just like the original and it was still on festive stationary. She also had the pictures of our family that we had sent. Apparently she had been studying these and rereading the letter, just as I had imagined. She had brought one pair of underwear, just in case her host family was unprepared, but otherwise had brought no other clothes. She did have a small book of some sort, as well as a bottle of perfume. It was a cute little bottle, with a spray button on the top. But it was gosh-awful smelling stuff and we wondered whether she knew it. After all, it could be that all Russian perfumes just smelled bad, right? Probably not, more likely this was just some cheap trinket that she had picked up, that was never meant to be very good. Of course, when you have very little, such trinkets can seem quite valuable. So, we did not let on that we were not impressed. It was sobering though, to think that this little girl had just traveled nearly 5,000 miles, to a place that she had never seen and where she did not speak the language, for a visit that would last nearly five weeks, with a family that she did not know, and this was all she had brought with her. It was a remarkable expression of trust, of that childlike faith that is mentioned in scripture. But it was also significant to us, in our American home and culture, where we have so much. This little girl had virtually nothing that was truly her own.

Of course, there was one thing that she did not unpack and that she kept entirely to herself and that was the little shopping bag that she had carried. Throughout the ride home and the tour of the house, she had held this little bag or kept it close by her side. What could be so important to a little girl who had so little? We could not imagine; however, we had learned quickly that whatever it was, we could not be trusted with it. So, we quit asking. Once in her own room, she did put it down but on the other side of the bed, between the bed and the wall, and she did not mention it again. We noticed but were content to leave her that bit of privacy. We had five weeks after all, plenty of time for us to gain her trust and for her to share her secrets.

Once we were home and once we had Yanna introduced to the house, we began to settle back into our routines. Cricket and Jaclyn helped Yanna get undressed, get a bath, and get into her pajamas. The boys, Chase and Christopher, and I went downstairs to the den, where we began watching TV. I remember this because I remember hearing the girls upstairs, turning on the water, walking back and forth between the rooms, and then finally emerging at the top of the stairs, with Yanna in her fresh, clean pajamas, her long, still wet, hair, and a smile that seemed to fill the room.

As best I can recall it now, we did not do much after that. It was getting late, after all. It was now well past 9:00 and it was Tuesday, a school night. Moreover, we were all tired from all the day's activities and excitement. We had told all of the jokes that we could tell; we had introduced Yanna to the house and to the dog and cat. She was unpacked and settled in and we were ready simply to unwind. So, the girls came downstairs, we sat and watched a little TV and then decided that it was time for bed. That meant it was time for prayers. The tradition at our house is that we pray with the children each night before they go to sleep. When everyone is there together, as they were that night, we like to form a circle, to hold hands and to recite the Lord's Prayer. Naturally, we included Yanna in the circle, regardless of whether she knew what we were doing or whether she understood the prayer.

As we ended our prayer and said "amen," Yanna opened her eyes and grew very excited. She began to say "Ya kristanskee, ya kristanskee!" She turned loose of our hands and ran to the stairs. We were all a bit confused, and mildly amused, by her outburst. This was more emotion and positive affect than she had displayed in all of the past two hours combined. She was clearly happy and clearly excited. She ran up the stairs, looking back at us while holding up a finger and saying "zhdad, zhdad" or "wait, wait." At that very moment, I turned to look at Cricket, who had tears welling up in her eyes. As she looked back at me, she smiled and silently mouthed, "she is adorable!" Cricket was right. We heard Yanna rummage about in her room for a few seconds, only to appear again in full sprint down the stairs, with a small book or card in her hands. Once back in the den, she plopped down on our large ottoman and repeated again, "ya kristanskee!" She then reached inside her pajamas and pulled out a small, silver cross. This cross was hanging on the string that I had seen around her neck in that first picture. She held the cross up for us to see and repeated again, "ya kristanskee!" Of course, she had recognized our prayer and was now telling us "I am Christian," too. In fact, she was showing us her cross, as if to prove it.

As we responded with acknowledgements of understanding and pleasure, she took the small book and showed it to us. It was a Russian Orthodox prayer book, with a Russian Orthodox icon on the front and writing on the inside. The writing, apparently, was a prayer. Yanna instructed, perhaps better she commanded, that we again close our eyes and bow our heads. She then read the prayer to us in Russian. At the conclusion we all said "amen;" we opened our eyes and looked at Yanna. She was beaming. For the moment at least, she was a part of our family, and she couldn't have been happier about it. We were all teary-eyed and smiling, too. What had started out with a rather bumpy and awkward introduction was now turning out great. She was adorable, just as we imagined her, and she was happy to be here with us. Cricket was thrilled; the children were happy, and I could not have been more content. We had our traditional group hug and everyone went off to bed, Yanna included. I don't really remember at this point, but I suspect that I slept very well.

Two days later, I wrote the second installment of my newsletter. I needed to report to everyone that Yanna was here, was safe and that the visit was off to a nice start. It was also fun to recount the events of those very first days. Naturally, we had hoped that things would go well and, so far at least, things were going even better than expected. And, so, I sent the following note to everyone on my mailing list.

December 14, 2006

I wanted to give you an update on Yanna. We picked her up at the airport Tuesday evening. By the time she got to the car, she had been traveling for 27 hours. So, she was tired, overwhelmed, and a little sad to leave her group. Also, not surprisingly, she wasn't feeling well. We gave her some Tylenol and simply took her home as quickly as we could.

Once home she began to feel better and to warm up. She loved her room and enjoyed unpacking her things. She went through the house to get to know the place and enjoyed turning on the Christmas lights and seeing her picture in various places. She especially loved meeting the dog (sabaka) and cat (kawshka). She took a bath, got into bed, and slept soundly until about 8:30 the next morning.

Here's a story you might enjoy. Before Christopher went to bed Tuesday night, we read him a devotional, as usual, and we all held hands and said the Lord's Prayer. Yanna was included, of course. Well, upon completing the prayer, Yanna looked up and exclaimed, "ya kristianskee" or "I am Christian" and she showed us a small cross, that she wears around her neck. She then ran up to her room and brought back a little prayer book, from which she recited the Lord's prayer in Russian!

She awoke from that first night's sleep and has been a non-stop joy ever since. We've been to Wal-Mart to buy clothes and other essentials. We had some photos taken of her and we had lunch at Chick-fil-A. I needed new sunglasses so we got Yanna a pair too. What a time that was, the two of us trying on sunglasses together. She played with the kids, shooting basketball with Chase and Christopher and jumping on the trampoline with Jaclyn. Finally, we had dinner after which she and Jaclyn watched a movie together. We then had our devotion and she went to bed.

Honestly, she is adorable and we are all smitten with her. She's learning some English and we're struggling to learn some "Rooskie." But communication hasn't been a problem. She's eaten most everything we've offered her (even when she doesn't really like it) and she is ever so polite and agreeable. We truly can sense God's anointing on her visit and we want to continue walking in that anointing. So we thank each of you for your prayers and we ask that you please continue to remember and to pray for Yanna.

Hopefully, you'll have the chance to meet her soon.

Blessings,

Allen

Change My Life

Although I keep referring to the visit as lasting five weeks, it was actually only 31 days, from December 12 to February 12. While 31 days is less than five weeks, in fact it is closer to four, it is still quite a long time. Long enough in fact that recounting all of the details of Yanna's visit would be practically impossible, not to mention potentially dull. Indeed, much of what we did during that first visit was rather mundane. We took walks, and we watched television. Yanna visited the schools and classes of the two younger children and joined Cricket on trips to the grocery store and on other shopping expeditions. We went to church, to various Christmas parties and even to a wedding. For the entire month, we simply went about our business. And we included Yanna in everything. So much of her time here was spent in very ordinary activities, doing the sorts of things that are underappreciated in the moment and even more quickly forgotten afterward. But there were also some truly memorable moments and those are the things that have endured in my memory and that I will share.

Perhaps the first of these occurred the next morning, the first full day of her visit. We all woke as we normally do and began preparing for school and work. As the kids and I were preparing to leave the house, I saw Yanna sitting peacefully at the top of the stairs, sleepy-eyed and still dressed in her pajamas. The activity in the house had woken her, and she had come out of her room; however, she just sat at the top of the stairs, watching the activity and perhaps wondering if she was dreaming. When I saw her, I called Cricket. Together, we looked up at Yanna and smiled. She smiled back and came down where Cricket greeted her with a hug. I then left on schedule, took the kids to school and went into the office.

Later that morning, I called home to see how things were going and, apparently, all was well. Yanna had eaten breakfast, toast with peanut butter, and spent some quiet time at home. Now, she and Cricket were going out to do some shopping. I decided to join them, first at Wal-Mart and then on several other stops. At Wal-Mart, we had Yanna's picture taken. We thought the picture was simply adorable and we still have copies of it. Yanna, however, did not like it at all. She still had that small mark from where she had bumped her nose on the tram at the airport and her hair was fixed in a way that was not to her liking. She also did not care for the jump suit that Cricket had selected for her to wear that day. Still, we thought she was cute and the process of getting the picture made was great fun. We took her to lunch at Chick-fil-A because we had read in her profile that she liked the chicken burgers served by McDonald's in Russia. So, we thought, she would surely love the nuggets at Chick-fil-A. As it turns out, she was somewhat underwhelmed by the experience. Oh, well. Nevertheless, she seemed to enjoy the time with us, even if she didn't enjoy the chicken quite as much as we had hoped. She did love the play area inside the Chick-fil-A though. So, we were off to successful start; things had picked up where they left off the night before.

After lunch, we decided to go to a nearby shopping center. I needed a new pair of sunglasses, and Cricket wanted to do some Christmas shopping. So, we all went into the store together, and I took Yanna with me to the rotating displays where the sunglasses were kept. Little did I know that my life was about to change forever.

As I described it earlier, it was a rather unremarkable set of circumstances. We were there in a small discount store that happened to carry a wide selection of sunglasses, at very low prices. I lose or destroy sunglasses frequently and, so, never spend much on them. Finding this store was a stroke of good fortune and I was, and still am, in there every few months. It's a small place, so I went straight to the display rack and began trying different frames. Yanna came with me and so she, too, began selecting various and different frames. Some were just plain silly and others were more serious. Still, as is often the case, most were not quite what either of us wanted, and, so, we began to have fun commenting on each selection. Of course, at this point Yanna had been here for less than 24 hours. She knew no English and I, apparently, knew absolutely no Russian, my efforts to the contrary aside. Still, we were able to communicate. I would put on a set of frames, and she would make a face. She would put on a pair and I would laugh. So, we were able to convey our thoughts and preferences well enough. Somewhere along the way I made my choice. Yanna, however, had not yet made hers. But, after a few more attempts, she put on a set of frames that suited her well. She was so cute in them, and she smiled that delightful smile, as she strained up towards me, looking for my reaction. And right there and right then, it happened.

As I described earlier, I simply knew that she was my daughter. Just as surely as Chase, Jaclyn and Christopher were all my children, too, Yanna was my daughter. Now, some will call it post hoc interpretation and say that I am simply remembering it as more than it was, that time and the significance of the process since have embellished my recollections. Others might say that I had really been committed to an adoption all along and that this was simply the moment it was confirmed in my mind and heart so that I allowed myself to accept it.

Well, I cannot tell people what to think. What I can do is offer my assurance that these sorts of interpretations are not correct. I was not looking to adopt a child. In fact, I had explicitly instructed Cricket, the kids and everyone else who knew about this that the "A word" was expressly banned from the lexicon of the Amason household. I had three beautiful children, a wonderful family and a great life. I was not about to be cornered into anything other than hosting. Moreover, I can assure you that this event was the key moment. In fact, as will be explained later, I told Yanna as much in a letter that I wrote to her later, during the long adoption process that followed. That moment, when I looked at her through those sunglasses, I felt the very same sensation as I had felt when I held each one of my other children for the very first time. In an unmistakable instant, as I simply looked at each of them, all four of them, I knew that they were mine. The only difference was that this time, I was in the middle of a store, standing there at the sunglasses case. It was overwhelmingly powerful; so much so that it startled me and nearly took away my breath. It also confused and upset me. And so, I decided to leave the store just then. We bought the sunglasses and left.

So what does one do with a revelation like this? I certainly couldn't tell Yanna. First, I could not speak her language. But, even if I could, I wasn't even yet sure that she liked me very much. And, even if she did, there was certainly no reason to think that she wanted me as a father. Besides, did she even need a father? As I explained earlier, many of the orphans in Russia are in fact social orphans. They may have parents and, perhaps, larger families; however, because of the social and economic conditions, they were orphans of circumstance. Maybe that was the case with Yanna. So, even if I could have told her, I wouldn't have. She was only nine years old after all and on the vacation of a lifetime. She could not possibly understand this burden.

So, I did absolutely nothing. I mean, what else was there to do? I couldn't tell Cricket; by agreement, we were not going to use the A-word. I wasn't going to tell the kids. The only discussions we had had with them on the subject were about hosting. Adoption was something that we never really discussed. It certainly wasn't the sort of thing that I was going to discuss with my colleagues or friends either. I am just not that open about private matters like this. Besides, what would I have said? No, I could not really talk about this with anyone. So, I prayed about it and just lived with it for a while because there was nothing else that I could do. Of course, the whole thing also left me somewhat sad. What was to become of Yanna? How was I going to send her home, knowing that I might never see her again? When the time came, how could I even send her home? Did I really have a choice? The irony here is that I had done the very thing that I wanted to avoid. I had backed myself into a corner after all; however, it was not at all the corner that I had feared. Here, I had made sure to assure myself, along with anyone else who asked, that I was uninterested in adopting a little girl and, yet, I was now fully convinced that this same little girl was in fact my daughter. So, like the visit itself, I simply went on.

She Called Me Poppy

The obvious part of the overall program and process is the actual hosting of the children. There were about 60 of them in total that winter, and each child went to his or her host family and lived, more or less independently. There

were events for all of the children, some of which I will
discuss later, but attendance at most of these was voluntary
and Yanna was more than happy to just spend time with us,
and we were happy to just spend time with her. A less
obvious part of the program, though, was the hosting of the
chaperones. The chaperones came in two groups, orphanage
workers and translators. The translators were from the home
countries of the children and were hired and their expenses
covered by NHFC. Their job was to attend all of the events
and to be on call, 24-hours a day, in the event that anyone,
whether a child, a family member, a chaperone or some
member of the program staff needed translation services.
Like the children, they lived with host families; however,
unlike the children, they were not expected to stay with these
families. So long as they were at the requisite events and
available by phone when needed, their time was their own.
And, because they all spoke English, they were able to enjoy
a variety of activities on their own. On the other hand, there
were the orphanage workers. Because the children were the
responsibility of the orphanages and because the orphanages
were administered by the Russian authorities, at what we
would view as the state level of government, those authorities
required that the children be accompanied by a number of
either orphanage or state workers. NHFC paid the expenses
of these workers too, however, they were representatives of
the government authorities and so were the final authority
should an issue come up with any one of the children. If a
child got sick, then one of the workers would have to approve

taking them to the doctor and prescribing them medication. If a child was injured and required a hospital visit, then a worker would have to approve any treatment. The workers were also available should there be problems, such as behavioral problems with a child or one of the families. So, they had to be here; however, if everything went well with the children, then the orphanage workers did not have much to do.

Moreover, none of these orphanage workers spoke English. They, too, lived with a host family but, unlike the translators, they were ill-equipped to entertain themselves. So, all of the families agreed to take a turn helping with chaperones. This was partly to share the burden and partly to market the program itself. Naturally, everyone wanted the authorities to think that this program was wonderful for the children, which it was; however, to demonstrate this positive effect, we wanted the workers to see the families, to see the children in the families, and to see everyone doing very well together. Armed with that knowledge, the workers would go back to Russia and report positively on all that they had seen and so enable the program to host more children in the future. And, so, like every other family, we had been asked to help by hosting, at some point, one of the three or four chaperones who had come with Yanna and the other Russian children. We understood the purpose and, so, had agreed to this during our orientation to the program. Thus, we made plans, during the early days of Yanna's visit, to host Lydia, the director of Yanna's orphanage.

Thankfully, LeAnn was more than happy to have us help with Lydia. As the director of the program, LeAnn wanted all of the chaperones to have a terrific time and to see as many of the families and children as possible. Beyond that, though, she wanted Lydia to be impressed. As an orphanage director, Lydia was in a position of great responsibility and influence. Lydia could promote the program within the Russian government or she could, with a phone call, shut it down. So, making a good impression on Lydia was important. Because we lived some distance away, nearly two hours from LeAnn and from the office of the program, by visiting us Lydia would see a different area and would meet some different people. Also, Athens is home to The University of Georgia and, in my position there, I could arrange a tour of the campus, a lunch at an on-campus restaurant, a visit to our international relations center where several Russian speakers worked, a stop at my office and, of course, a stop at the famous football stadium. I had even located a translator who I hired for the afternoon to accompany us on the tour. This is exactly the sort of thing that LeAnn wanted for Lydia and, so, she agreed to let us host Lydia during the very next week, the first full week of Yanna's visit.

The logistics went something like this; I would drive from our home in Watkinsville, a suburb of Athens, Georgia, to Acwroth, Georgia, a small town in the Atlanta suburbs, about 45 minutes north and west of downtown, pick up Lydia and bring her back to Athens, where we would meet Cricket,

Yanna and my hired translator for lunch on the UGA campus. Under normal conditions, driving from Athens to Acworth should take about two hours, or maybe a little less. On this day, though, there had been an accident so it took nearly three hours. That was embarrassing. Thankfully, though, Lydia seemed not to mind; in fact, she seemed rather pleased to see me again.

By the time I picked her up, it was nearly 10:00 in the morning. I had left home around 7:00 before Yanna was up. So, I had never told Yanna where I was going or what we were planning. I am not sure what I would have told her anyway, since my Russian vocabulary by this time was still limited to about three words – and even those I seemed to mispronounce. So, Yanna had no idea what was in the works. Sometime around 9:00, she quizzed Cricket on the plans for the day and my whereabouts. Cricket spoke even less Russian than I but she was somehow able to convey to Yanna that I had gone to Atlanta and that I would return soon with Lydia. Upon hearing this, Yanna got very excited, much like she was excited on that first night when she told us that she was a Christian.

She was very animated and excited and asked Cricket again and again about the plan. So, not long after I picked up Lydia, Cricket called me to tell me all of this. What made it all so special, though, was how Yanna discussed it. Once she finally understood, she asked Cricket "Lydia [and] Poppy?" That is what was so important and that is what Cricket called to tell me; she called me Poppy! Now, looking back on it, this seems a bit silly. I mean, what else was she supposed to call me... Mr. Amason? She probably did not even know my first name, and I doubt she would have used it anyway. So, Poppy was certainly logical and certainly as good as anything else. But you also have to remember that it was not rational analysis that led me to sense that Yanna was my daughter. Rather, it was something that I knew in my spirit. It was also something that I had not yet shared with anyone. So, when I heard that she had called me Poppy, you can imagine the wave of emotion that stirred. So, between that and the fact that I was now nearly an hour behind schedule, I drove back to Athens very quickly.

The visit with Lydia went very well. She seemed to genuinely appreciate the somewhat official nature of the tour, with the translator and all. She marveled at the football stadium, even if she had no idea what American college football was. She really engaged the people at the international relations center and talked with them in detail about Russian politics and about her impressions of the U.S. and of UGA. Interestingly, one of the women who worked at the international relations center began talking with Yanna. Because the translator was still with us and was working for me, he continued to translate all that was said for my benefit. This worker was simply being polite and making conversation; and she said to Yanna, "your hair is very pretty. Who fixed it for you?" Yanna's response, "my mama." Now, this just came out of Yanna's mouth with little thought; however, the moment she heard the translator relay it to me, she shot me a worried glance. Was it okay for her to call Cricket mama? Had she overstepped her bounds? Again, what else what was she supposed to call her? So, I did the only reasonable and appropriate thing; I pretended not to notice and the issue dropped.

But I did notice and I still remember that brief moment. All these years later, I still remember it well. The reason is because, while it seems a minor thing, it was really quite important, and not just for me. You see, had Yanna not thought it important, then she would not have given me that uneasy look. It was just a glance and it lasted just a second. But it was enough to convince me that Yanna knew very well what she was doing. Just as I wanted to adopt her, so was she also beginning to adopt us. She was in fact thinking of Cricket as her mama and of me as her father. This little orphan girl now had a mama and poppy. And while she thought it was only for a short time, I knew it was for much more. If only it had been that simple.

Normal Everyday Life

As mentioned, I make no claim to remember every detail of that first visit. Most of the time, we simply shared our normal everyday life together. I can remember Yanna waiting for Jaclyn and Christopher to come home from school. She loved to jump on the trampoline with Jaclyn. She didn't really care for American food but she seemed to love dinner time, when the family would sit down together to eat. She loved doing puzzles; she loved playing with the dog and the cat, and she loved the ritual that we developed around bedtime. At the time, both Christopher and Jaclyn went to bed at 9:00 on school nights and 10:00 otherwise. To us that seemed reasonable and we gave Yanna the same boundaries, explaining them to her carefully. The ritual was always the same; starting sometime between 8:00 and 8:30, we would start getting the kids ready. They would shower, brush their teeth and put on their pajamas and do the stuff necessary to get ready for bed. We would then all sit down together, read our bible study from a children's bible, say our prayers and then pack everyone off to sleep.

All of our children always enjoyed this process thoroughly, as did Yanna. Well, that is right up until the moment when she was to actually go to bed. At this moment, she would work vigorously to convince us that she simply was not sleepy. I would say, "come Yanna, time for sleepy sleepy." More or less on cue, she would respond, "no sleepy sleepy…" and proceed to do just about anything she could to make us laugh and so distract us from the fact that it was time for bed. We could not tell whether she understood that she was being disobedient, whether she thought she really could talk us out of putting her to bed, or whether she realized just how cute she was and so was putting on this act for our benefit. Most likely, it was a mixture of all these things. Regardless though, it soon became a part of the routine and an inside joke among our family. To this day, we will still sometimes say to one another, "no sleepy sleepy," in our made up Russian accents, and we will remember that first visit.

There was the time we sent Yanna to a basketball game with Chase. Recall that in her bio sketch, we had read that she liked basketball. Truth be told, if she any feelings about the sport, they were decidedly negative. How that got into her bio in the first place, I'll never know. She now claims that it was none of her doing. Regardless, we thought she liked basketball and that she would like attending a major college basketball game with Chase. So, we made plans for her to go. We had season tickets and Chase was going anyway. So, he would take Yanna. Well, when I informed her of the plan, she responded with an emphatic no. So, we tried the soft approach; we told her what a good time she would have. We told her that it was a big coliseum, with a big crowd and top-notch basketball. We told her that Chase was going and that he wanted to take her with him. Surely that would do the trick. Unfortunately, we were not that lucky.

Yanna only grew angrier and angrier as we reasoned with her about it. She crossed her arms and proclaimed that she was not going. Of course, she still did not speak any English; so proclamations of this type were something of an emergent process. Still, like watching a thunderstorm form on the distant horizon, we could sense what was building. This particular storm came to a head when I physically picked Yanna up and placed her in Chase's car. She was kicking and screaming. This was clearly not going the way that we had hoped it would go. So, I shifted my strategy and adopted a harder approach. I left her in the car and ran back into the house and to my computer, where I typed the following note:

> *"You are going to the game with Chase. If you do not behave, you will not be allowed to play with the computer for the entire week."*

Yanna loved playing games on the computer, and, so, this seemed a reasonable sanction and one that should have the desired effect. Using an online program that I had found, I quickly translated my note into Russian, printed a copy of it, and took it outside where Yanna was seething in the backseat of Chase's car. I handed it to her and she read it. She handed it back, acknowledged my instruction and changed her expression. She still was not positive but at least she was not quite so negative. She was no longer screaming "no," and she was no longer trying to get out of the car.

Now, Chase had seen all of this. So, I wouldn't have blamed him at all if he simply decided to drop the whole thing and stay home. Being a good sport, though, and a real basketball fan, he decided to go on with the plan, and Cricket and I spent the next three hours feeling sorry for him and worrying how it was going.

I'm not sure what I was expecting upon their return, but I surely was not expecting what I saw. They arrived home, and Chase carried a smiling and laughing Yanna from the car into the house. She was holding a stuffed animal and a drink cup. They were carrying on as if they had known and loved one another for years and as if they had just enjoyed one of many of the good times that they often enjoyed together. Like a good big brother, with a loving little sister, they came into the house without the slightest hint of the earlier drama. Upon asking him, Chase explained that once they left the house, Yanna became much more agreeable. And, then, once at the arena, he bought her a toy and a drink, and they enjoyed the game as we had always hoped they would.

I remember one day my father and step-mother had come to visit. They spent a couple days with us, doing nothing in particular but visiting, giving the kids their Christmas gifts and meeting Yanna. The memorable part of the visit came just before they left. We all decided to go out for breakfast and so we went together to a local, old-fashioned diner in downtown Athens. Yanna had been to restaurants with us, but, like most children, she needed some help ordering. Not only did she not speak or read the language, but American food is substantially different from Russian food. So, we would have some sort of discussion with her, as best we could, and then we would order on her behalf. Sometimes, we would get it right and she would love it; other times not so much. By now, though, we were all used to the routine.

This particular day, I ordered her pancakes. Pancakes are harmless enough, and I really thought she would like them. Pancakes are also common in Russia, although they are made and served somewhat differently. Well, the orders came and everyone dug in, except Yanna. She looked at the pancakes on her plate like a high school biology student might look at the animal they were about to dissect. She poked them, smelled them, tilted her head to assess them from a different perspective. But what she didn't do was taste them. So, I picked up the syrup and offered to put some on for her. "Nyet," she said forcibly... "ketchup." What? Did she really intend to put ketchup on her pancakes? "No, Yanna, you don't put ketchup on pancakes," I said. "Yes, ketchup," she said. So, I handed her the bottle and she absolutely soaked those pancakes in ketchup. Then, and to her credit, she actually ate about half of them... yuck. To be sure, she didn't much like them either. But, let me tell you two things about Yanna; she is lovable, and she is stubborn. So, she ate the pancakes, ketchup and all.

Out of the Bag and On the Table

There was Christmas movie night and the family meeting that coincided with it. This is a fun family tradition and a great memory, but it was also an especially big deal, as I will explain. First, the background is this; the hosting agency required that all the children be present at an afternoon gathering at a church in a suburb north of Atlanta. The gathering was called "America 101" and was designed to be a time for the children to ask questions, to tell their counselors how things were going, for the hosting agency to tell them some things about American culture and traditions around Christmas and just for everyone to check in. Also, while there, the children made Christmas gifts for their host families. It was important to the hosting agency, and, so, we built our schedule around it.

As I described earlier, we have this tradition called Christmas movie night. Well, this time we organized the event around Yanna's America 101 gathering. We would go into Atlanta, grab a bite of lunch, take Yanna to the church, find some way to kill the four hours between 1:00 and 5:00, then pick her up and head downtown, in time for our dinner reservation. The plan was perfect. What I didn't count on was the holiday traffic being so thick that I ended up running late. Then, to compound the problem, I tried to run around the traffic by taking a secondary road, only to find that road construction along this alternative route made me even later. The long and short of this was that we didn't get to stop for lunch and we still didn't get Yanna to the gathering until nearly 1:30.

Now, if you feel sorry for Yanna, don't; they had all manner of snack food at the gathering. For the rest of the family though, we were starved. So, we decided to find a spot where we could grab a bite. As luck would have it, just a short distance away was a Moe's and a basket of nachos would be just what the doctor ordered. Of course, there was also more to it than just this. You see, by now Yanna had been with us for almost two weeks. While no one had talked about adoption, as we had agreed, we had all thought about it. Somehow, I knew that this little girl was my daughter; but I had yet to reveal that to anyone. I could tell that Cricket was hopelessly in love, but she had yet to talk about adoption either. It was hard to tell with the kids. They were clearly very fond of Yanna and were enjoying her visit. But, what would they think about adopting her? What we needed was a time to sit and discuss it, as a family, and this particular restaurant, on this particular day, was just the spot.

So, we ordered up two baskets of nachos and a round of drinks, funny how I still remember that, and we sat down to discuss it. There was no agenda for this meeting, and I wasn't quite sure how to start the conversation. As it turned out, though, no agenda was necessary; Chase simply broke the ice the moment we sat down. "All right" he said, "we are going to adopt her, aren't we?" Bang! With that the "A" word was out of the bag and on the table. We talked for a long while about the logistics of adoption and about the stress it would place on our family. Cricket, Chase and Christopher were all on board, no matter the cost. But I remember looking at Jaclyn and seeing her begin to cry. I asked her what was wrong, and I felt terrible as she explained that, while she loved Yanna, she did not want a sister. She was my little girl; she was the only daughter in our family and she simply could not bear the thought of another little girl calling me daddy. This was a hard thing for her, and my heart ached for the pain it was causing. At the same time, it was the right thing to do. We all loved Yanna, and we couldn't simply send her back to Russia to continue living in an orphanage without at least trying to bring her into our family. We had to see if adoption was at least possible, and, if it was possible, then we had to pursue it. As I told Jaclyn, at some point as she grew older and more mature, she would see that this was something that we had to do. However, if we waited to start the process until she had that revelation, then it would be too late. So, we had to start now. She struggled with the idea, but she also understood. So, we finished our nachos, finished our meeting, and left to pick up Yanna. Oddly, we still couldn't use the "A" word, only now for a different reason.

The rest of the night was something of a blur; dinner at Maggiano's, one of our favorite Italian restaurants, the show by Cirque du Soleil, the ride home, Yanna proclaiming, "no sleepy, sleepy" even as she slept in my arms as I carried her to bed. The whole thing seemed like a dream. We were actually going to adopt Yanna, or we were at least going to try. All of our children were home, healthy and happy and life was good.

Soon thereafter it was Christmas Day. While that day was ostensibly the highlight of the trip, I recall very little about it. Yanna was delighted, of course. She received the same bounty of gifts as our other children, with some clothes, toys and other knick-knacks piled together in her "spot" on the floor or stuffed into her stocking. She also gave us some gifts. This is where we found out what she had been protecting in that carefully guarded shopping bag that I mentioned earlier. It was a beautiful origami bird, made from hundreds of folds. She delivered it to us in an enormous red stocking. She made the stocking at the America 101 meeting she had attended. She was just one of the family, receiving and giving gifts, sitting on laps of her mama and poppy, brothers and sister, enjoying all the day had to offer. The most touching moment, though, came when Yanna gave her Christmas gift to Jaclyn. It was a yellow card that she had made herself. On the top, it depicted a black and broken heart; on the bottom was a red and whole heart, held by a number of hands and arms. Somehow, Yanna managed to explain that these pictures represented her own heart. The black and broken heart was hers, before she met us. The red and whole heart was her heart now. The hands, of course, were ours. Without knowing it, we had mended her broken and lonely heart and now she was healthy and whole, with us.

It was a beautiful moment and a beautiful and mature expression from such a young child. It was humbling and touching, and we all began to cry, Jaclyn harder than anyone. But it was also bittersweet, as we couldn't help but remember that Yanna would be going back to Russia soon. Like it or not, this world, this beautiful family and this wonderful dream that we had been living was as artificial as it was temporary. It would last for only a few more days and then the real world, the cold and cruel world of hard reality, would return. Yanna would go back to an orphanage and to a world that we simply did not know and could barely image, leaving us with just memories. The weight of this realization made this gift all the more poignant, and it gave urgency to our effort.

Christmas day ended when my mother and stepfather, who had been visiting for the day, left to go home. As tradition had it, our kids went home with 'Nana' for a short, after-Christmas visit. Well, as soon as Yanna understood that this was an option, she ran upstairs and began packing her suitcase. It really was cute; she pulled out the pink roll-aboard case that she had just gotten for Christmas, and she began stuffing it with everything she owned. She was going to Nana's with her brothers and sister, and she could not have been happier about it. To be honest, I was apprehensive, but I gave in after some persuasion from Nana, Cricket and Yanna. It was the day after Christmas that I wrote the next installment on my newsletter.

December 26, 2006

It's been a while since our last update but, as you can imagine, we've been kept rather busy.

Yanna is doing splendidly. We went into Atlanta for a family night on the town. We went shopping at Lenox Square, had dinner at Maggiano's, and saw Cirque du Soleil's Corteo. Later that week, we went to Stone Mountain, where we rode the train, took the tram to the top of the mountain, and watched the laser show. She loved every minute of it all, and so did we.

We've been to several Christmas parties. One of those, on Christmas Eve, was near Stone Mountain, at the home of my cousin, Kappy. Kappy's house is spectacular and has an indoor pool. So Yanna, Christopher, and Jaclyn went swimming and had a great time. Yanna slept with

Jaclyn Christmas Eve. We all got up around 8:00; we opened some presents and then went to breakfast at Waffle House. We then returned and finished opening our gifts. She was delighted throughout.

One of the gifts that Yanna gave us was a hand-crafted bird, made of thick card paper. It was made from pieces of paper, folded hundreds of times; it must have taken many hours and she brought it with her from Russia. It is absolutely amazing. She also made a card for Jaclyn. She drew two hearts, one broken and black, the other whole and red. Yanna explained that these were her hearts. The first was her old one, before she came to us. The second was her heart now. The hands around the hearts are those of our family, taking her broken heart and putting back together. We all cried at hearing this.

Tonight, Yanna has gone with the kids to my mother's house. She was really excited it, so she must be feeling very comfortable and secure with us. My mother is a social worker, who works with foster children and families, and she thinks Yanna is very lovable, stable, and well adjusted.

As an example of that, here's a story from earlier this week: Cricket and Yanna were leaving Kroger and walked past the Salvation Army kettle. Cricket explained that donations helped poor families and children and Yanna wanted to give something. So Cricket tried to hand her some money. Yanna though did not want to take any money from Cricket. Instead, she wanted to give money of her own. When she arrived, we gave Yanna a small purse. In it, we put some tissues, a pack of gum, and 35 cents. It was just a token, to make Yanna feel that she had something of her *own. Yet, it was this $.35 that she wanted to give away. Somehow, she knew that she was safe and secure and that she could give away what little she had to those who needed it more. How many of us could be so generous?*

Amidst all this however, we've not lost sight of the big picture and of the decision that we soon must make. We are falling in love with this little girl and could easily see ourselves becoming her "forever family." Yet, it is God's will that matters. And so, we ask you to pray diligently. Pray for God's direction and will to be confirmed to us. Pray for God's favor and intervention throughout the process. But mostly, pray for Yanna. As much as we may love her, God loves her more. He formed her and called her by name and He has a plan for her life. While we would love to be a part of that plan, our prayer is that God's will be fulfilled and that she will have life and have it abundantly.

Merry Christmas,

Allen

One thing you may notice is that I did not made public our intention to adopt. Remember, this was after our family meeting and after we had made our decision; however, we had not yet done anything about it, at least not formally. The truth is, we didn't really know what we were supposed to do. Okay, so we wanted to adopt Yanna; well, that's all well and good but just exactly how were we to start that process? Truth be told, we didn't have a clue. And, so, we turned to the only person that we thought we could ask, LeAnn, the director of the hosting organization.

Unfortunately though, LeAnn was busy with the hosting program and the 60 or so children for whom she was responsible. She was also busy with families from previous hosting programs who were now in the midst of the adoption process. So we wrote to her, asking what we should do. Wait, was the answer. So, we called and explained our sense of urgency. Again, wait, was the answer. Now, you have to understand that calling me impatient is like calling the Biblical flood a spring shower. I do not wait. I pride myself on my ability to make things happen, to move faster, to think and act quicker, and to do more, much more, than most people think possible. I am one of those people who approaches a traffic intersection while trying to judge the slowest car around me, so as to get in the lane opposite of it. I count the people and items in the shopping baskets ahead of me as I choose a line at the supermarket, so as to choose the shortest, and I gladly pay more to park nearer the entrance at the airport, so as not to endure the long walk to my car or the interminable wait for off-site transportation. Put simply, I abhor waiting in lines and am irritated when I am forced to slow down for the group. Yet, LeAnn was telling me, slow down for the group. Hence, while our adoption process had set sail in our hearts, in practice, it was still tied to the dock.

And so the days passed, we took a short trip, picking up Jaclyn, Christopher and Yanna from my mother's house and heading to Washington, D.C., to visit family. Along the way, we stopped at our lake cabin, where Yanna and Christopher wrestled and jumped on two large bean bags.

Yanna also managed to walk directly into our sliding glass door, twice. Poor thing, she had never seen a solid glass door before and simply forgot it was there. And so she smacked her face and head against the glass. We felt terrible for her, but it was still rather funny. We spent New Year's in Washington, and we did a little site seeing. From a distance, you would have never known that we weren't one big happy family. Of course, as you got closer, you would hear Yanna speaking Russian and us speaking English and so you would quickly realize that the appearance was deceiving.

As our visit with family in Maryland wound down, the reality began to settle in that Yanna's visit was coming to a close, and, so, we cherished every minute with her all the more. The prospect of sending her back to Russia was heartbreaking. She was a member of our family and one of our children. How could anyone expect us simply to give her up? We dealt with the stress as best we could, largely by simply ignoring it and choosing not to think about the prospect of her leaving. We just enjoyed each day and tried not to worry about the immediate future. We also decided to begin sharing our intentions with our prayer partners. We wanted and needed their support, of course. But more than that, beginning to talk about the adoption was therapeutic for us. Somehow, it just seemed that, if we were talking about and working on the adoption, the process of sending Yanna back would be less difficult. And so, it was on this family visit that I wrote the next installment of my newsletter and revealed our desire to adopt.

January 3, 2007

Thank you for praying for Yanna. Her visit has been such a blessing; it's hard to imagine how it could have gone any better. It's also hard to believe that Yanna has been here for three weeks and that she will be going home in ten days. She has captured our hearts and feels like a part of our family. So, after much prayer, discussion, and careful consideration, we have decided to move forward with adoption.

Now, it is very important that she know nothing of this. So, please do not mention it to her. She knows that she is going back to Russia on the 12th and while she is sad about that, she understands and accepts it. So, until the proper time, that is all she needs to know. In the meantime, Cricket and I will be working diligently to push this process forward and to bring Yanna back home. So, please continue praying, for us, for Yanna, and for a process that goes smoothly and quickly and so testifies to God's anointing on this little girl's place in our family.

Since my last note, Yanna has been busy. She's been for a visit to my mother's house, in Cornelia Georgia, as well as a trip to our lake house in Hartwell. She also took a trip to Washington / Baltimore, to visit family there. Along the way, she saw the Capitol, the White House, the Smithsonian, and several of the monuments on the Washington Mall. She went to the Inner Harbor in Baltimore, did some shopping at the Baltimore Galleria, and went ice skating. She celebrated New Year's with us there, watching the ball drop on television and watching fire works around the neighborhood.

Through it all she was delighted and delightful. She got along well with her new "aunt, uncle, and cousins" and hugged them all when we said goodbye. She spent her first night ever in a hotel and marveled at the key card that opened the door. She loved the video game Dance, Dance Revolution and played it over and over. At the lake we built a campfire and she cooked hotdogs and sang Christmas carols while bundled up against the cold. She played with Christopher and Jaclyn on our long car trips, enjoying stops at McDonald's and at various gas stations. All the while, she worked to learn more English and to teach us some Russian.

Of course, these experiences will be good memories for her to take back to Russia. How I wish that she did not have to go. As it stands, though, this is the process to which we committed and it is for the best. She will go back to a safe place and a place she knows well. She'll settle into her routine and reconnect with her friends and caregivers. Then, Lord willing and when the time is right, she'll be told about the adoption. So, please pray that we will stand up well to the challenge of sending her back. Pray for peace for Cricket and I, and for comfort for Yanna. Pray that she will travel safely and that the time will pass quickly. Pray that she will be settled and happy back in familiar surroundings and that she'll be thrilled when the times comes for her to hear our news. We love her dearly and we want to be her forever family. So, please agree to pray with us that God will bring that about and bring it about quickly.

Blessings,

Allen

The final ten days of Yanna's visit was again something of a blur. We were trying very hard to be normal for her, to keep a normal routine and not let on how distressed and sad we were. It was difficult, but we managed. We were also, finally, beginning to make some progress on the adoption. Step one, we learned, was to get a home study and, thankfully, the hosting agency required that we complete a home study before we could qualify as hosts. So, that was pretty much done. I say pretty much because there were a few more details that would need to be added before our home study was sufficient for an adoption application. So we scheduled an appointment with the same social worker who had done the home study to begin with and spent some time with her, filling in the blanks. Of course, we took Yanna with us on this visit. We connected it with a trip into Atlanta that we had been planning anyway. And, for all Yanna knew, we were simply visiting a friend and we were happy to allow her to continue in that belief, with no earthly idea of what we were doing.

To be perfectly candid about it, I think we did a pretty good job of managing this whole thing without ever letting on what we were doing. We even developed a code name for it; we used this code word every time we needed to discuss adoption when Yanna was near. We called it "project platypus." So, when we were scheduling the trip in to Atlanta, to meet the social worker, we would simply say, "well, we'll do the platypus visit and then go to dinner." Even if she managed to figure out what platypus meant, which was unlikely, she would never figure out what we were really doing. The whole thing became quite amusing.

Here's a funny story from that first "project platypus" visit. As mentioned, we had gone into Atlanta for the day anyway. We were going out to dinner and were then going to a hockey game. The game was a group event, organized by NHFC as a special treat for the children that would soon be going home. We likely would not have gone to the game at all but had received a call from the social worker about the need to schedule an appointment; she had been contacted by LeAnn and told of our plans to adopt. She explained that our first step was to add some additional details to our original home study. This would involve some in-depth interviews and the provision of some more in-depth information. Since the social worker had already been to our home, we could have this additional meeting at her office, which was in a suburb west of Atlanta.

So, like so many other times, we packed up the family in the minivan and set off. The plan was to go to the social worker's office, which was in her home. We would each do our respective interviews in her home office, while the rest of us milled about in her den, or went to a nearby shopping mall. We simply told Yanna that were visiting a friend. She certainly wouldn't know any better nor would she particularly care. And, other than the fact that it was cold, rainy and generally miserable, everything went according to plan. The funny part came later, once we had finished with the social worker and were on our way back to downtown

Atlanta for the hockey game. We were all in the car, riding quietly amidst the rain and traffic when Christopher pipes up from his spot in the backseat and screams "I've got it!" Got what, we asked? "I've found a word that rhymes with orange... it's door hinge. Get it? Or-ange... dor-inge?" He was completely serious.

Well, after a brief but punctuated silence, we all just burst out laughing. And when I say laughing, I mean laughing. We were howling and it was all I could do to keep the car on the road. Well, Yanna had watched all this with perfect innocence and confusion. And given that she did not speak English, she had no idea why we were all laughing so. So, she asked Christopher, as best she could, who tried to explain, as best he could. The only problem was that, somewhere along the way, he used the words "door hinge." Not knowing what that meant, she took offense and said to Christopher "you're a door hinge." Christopher shot right back, "no, you're a door hinge." At that, Yanna took terrible offense, shut down all communication, crossed her arms and began to cry.

Now, we had seen this behavior once before, several weeks prior. We had insisted that Yanna wear her nametag when we took her shopping. It wasn't just us; NHFC required all parents to insure that no child was ever in public without a name tag, worn around their neck, explaining that they did not speak English and providing the names and phone numbers of the hosting parents. Well, Yanna hated the nametag and was furious with us for making her wear it, so furious in fact that she completely shut down contact with us. There was no talking, no sound at all, no eye contact, no touching; a stuffed animal would have been more animated and friendly. The only indication of any life was the angry glare in her eyes. On the first instance, she held that countenance for more than an hour, despite our best efforts to draw her out. Well, on this day in Atlanta, after that harmless exchange with Christopher, the switch flipped again and she shut down again. It wasn't until we had parked the car and were walking into the arena that she finally explained what had happened. "Kreestofer called me a door-ange," she explained, after some coaxing. We showed her what a door hinge was, explained to her that the whole thing was a joke that had nothing to do with her and suddenly, just as quickly as she had turned herself off, she turned right back on. Afterward, we enjoyed a perfectly delightful evening, watching a professional hockey game, meeting some of the other hosting families and children, we even finished the night off with a visit to the top of the Peachtree Plaza Westin, a 73 story hotel with a revolving observation level.

After that outing, the days passed rather quickly. The social worker completed the home study and sent us the final report. We took that report and put it together with a bunch of other stuff, like another criminal background check, our fingerprints, our marriage license and birth certificates, proof of residency, information on our home, et cetera, and we put it together with a long form that we completed from the USCIS, which stands for the United States Citizenship and

Immigration Service. This package was a request, to the U.S. government, to certify us as good people, who could adopt a foreign child. This form is the first thing a foreign government wants to see in an adoption dossier. So, until you have an approved I-600 form, which is what it's called, you cannot even approach a foreign government to begin an adoption.

To get an I-600, you file this thick package of materials. Then, you wait for a letter. That letter tells you that you have been approved to the next step, which is yet another set of fingerprints, taken this time in digital form, at a USCIS facility. The letter also gives you the time and date of your appointment. Now, if you can't make that time and that day, then you've got to reschedule, and that's real trouble. It could set you back a week; it could set you back two months. So, it's best to just keep an open calendar throughout the process.

Before we could worry about any of that, though, we needed to get the application filed. So, we completed the form quickly, got all that other stuff collected, copied and notarized, put them together with the home study and got ready to send it all in; we planned to send it FEDEX because, as the old commercial used to say, it absolutely, positively had to get there. What is interesting about all this is that we finished this first round of paperwork just a day or two before Yanna was to leave. On that day, Cricket and I decided to have lunch together and to bring Yanna. The other children were already back in school and Chase had already returned to college. So, it was a bittersweet little outing for the three of us. And there, over lunch, Cricket and I sifted through the forms one last time, signed and put them in the FEDEX envelope. We then went to the nearest FedEx drop box, where we handed the packet to Yanna and asked her to drop it in the receptacle. To this day, we still think it's neat that Yanna was the one to mail the adoption application. Of course, she had no idea what was in the packet or what she had just done. She simply thought it was fun to drop the packet in the box and be out doing something with her mommy and poppy.

To us, though, it was important. Yanna was going back to Russia in a just a couple of days, and we could not bear the thought of it. This was our daughter, and, even though she did not yet know it, we did. Nevertheless, she was going to have to leave us, for an indefinite period of time. What is more, she was going to leave without the slightest hint of what was going on. We were going to have to send her back, knowing that she thought she would never return and never see us again. It was heartbreaking, and the stress of it was almost unbearable. So, this one little gesture really meant a lot. We hoped, somehow, she would figure out that we wanted her for always and that she would reason that we would do whatever it took to make that so. Whether she realized any of this though, the fact was that Yanna was leaving us in just two days, and I was gripped by a grief that was darker and stronger than anything I had ever felt. And so, it was about this time that I wrote the next installment of my newsletter.

January 9, 2007

Before she even arrived, we knew that Yanna would go back to Russia this Friday, January 12th. What we did not know then was how difficult it was going to be to say goodbye. This has been a special season, a blessing beyond measure, everything we prayed it would be, and more. And we give praise and thanks to God for it.

Yanna has had a good week. We went to Atlanta, for a Thrashers game; after which we walked through Centennial Olympic Park and then went to the Sundial, atop Peachtree Plaza. We went to a UGA gymnastics meet and Yanna understood and followed the competition well. She went bowling and to Chuck E. Cheese, with another little girl who spoke Russian and they had a great time together. She also saw microwave popcorn for the first time. While that is an experience that many of us take for granted, rest assured it was a true event for Yanna. She made two trips to the dentist, after which she was given a clean bill of oral health. And she went to the eye doctor, where she was found to be 20/20 and in excellent shape.

In every way, it has been a great trip and if Yanna were to leave for Russia, never to return, we would still count ourselves blessed to have known her. Yet, we want more. We want to be Yanna's forever family, to provide for her and to care for her. We want to bring her up in the love and security of our home and to provide a foundation on which she can build a future and a life. We want nothing less than for her to have life, to have it abundantly, and to have it here, with us.

*So, we ask that you continue to pray. Even as she
prepares to leave, we ask that you to pray
earnestly for her return. We ask that you pray for
us and for her, as Friday will be a difficult day.
Pray for her comfort and peace as she returns and
pray that God will move miraculously to bring
Yanna home to us quickly and easily.*

*Yanna has captured our hearts and we love her
dearly. So, we thank God for her and for you.
And we thank you for your prayers on her behalf.*

Blessings,

Allen

The End of the Beginning

The day before Yanna was to leave, we travelled with
her to Atlanta one final time for the going away party. This
was an event, hosted by NHFC, for all the children and
families in the hosting program. It is a fun time; everyone
eats, then we play games and socialize. There are two or
three reasons for the get together. First, it allows the
families, many of whom now know one another, to enjoy one
last fun time out with their hosted children. Second, it allows
the children to reconnect with their friends and caregivers
from the orphanage. Many of them would not have seen
their friends for weeks now, other than at these organized
functions. So, the kids were happy to get back together and
swap stories. Finally, it provided an opportunity for the
NHFC leaders to go over the details of the next day at the
airport. We were told what time to arrive, what we could and

couldn't pack in our children's luggage, how we would go about checking our children in for their flight, and other sorts of logistical instructions. We were also told about how long it would take to get everyone organized and ready to go to the gate and so about how much time we would have to say our goodbyes. All in all, it was a useful and fun evening but it was also a painful one. We did not want Yanna to go, and we certainly did not want to spend a lot of time discussing the details of her departure.

For her part, Yanna enjoyed the party completely. The moment we arrived, she jumped out of the car and ran to the building. She did not want me holding her, or even holding her hand. I don't know if she was embarrassed to seem too close to us or if she was simply just too excited to be back with her friends. Either way, it was a joy to see her so excited, even if we couldn't share in the excitement ourselves. Over the course of the evening, she ate with her friends, talking and laughing with them continuously, but she also warmed back up to us. During the games, she stayed with our family and, as the evening wore on, we wanted more and more for Cricket or me to hold her. When the time came to leave, she did so happily, climbing back into our car just like our other children and then singing along to the radio with them for the whole ride home. She was so incredibly happy, and we were happy for her. That said, we were devastated at the prospect of sending her back and so dreaded the arrival of the next day.

Friday morning we awoke as usual. The kids went off to school, and I went off to work. Chase had come home from college the night before, so that he could accompany us to the airport, just as he had the day that Yanna arrived. We were to be at the airport by 1:00 p.m. so that Yanna could be checked in and reconnected to her group in time for the whole group to make it through security and to the gate in time for their 4:30 flight. It was a mirror image of our schedule on the day she arrived. Our moods were a mirror image as well. Everything ran slowly and sadly and nothing about the day was exciting. I came home from the office around 11:00 to load up and begin the trip. The moment I walked in the door, Yanna ran and jumped into my arms. I simply broke down. Tough as she was, Yanna wiped away my tears and said "no, Poppy, no." I got up, we loaded Yanna's luggage into the minivan, and we left.

The ride itself was fun; it was one final outing that the whole family was taking together. But we all knew that we wouldn't come back from it together. Still, we tried to make the most of the ride. We stopped along the way at Dairy Queen for ice cream. We did some joking and laughing, and we tried to talk to Yanna about the future. Of course, we couldn't tell her about the adoption, but we could tell her that we loved her and that we always would. We told her that we would write and that we might visit one day. We had already made plans for Cricket to join a mission team from our church that would soon visit orphanages in St. Petersburg. And the team was planning to visit Yanna's orphanage. Still we couldn't promise anything other than a brief visit. Once or twice along the way, Yanna actually cried and asked if she could stay, or at least come back. Again, we couldn't promise anything; all we could do was say that we hoped so.

We had been given Yanna's passport and ticket, and, so, we took her to the counter and got her checked in without incident. We put the Russian nametag NHFC had prepared for us on her new, pink suitcase, and we got that checked in as well. We had not yet seen any of her friends, and, so, we went for one last meal together, as a family. We tried to recapture the magic from our other meals together, but it just wasn't there. Every time before, when we would go out together, there was joy, excitement and laughter. This time, though, we just sat and ate in the middle of the crowded terminal, watching the clock constantly so as not be late but dreading the thought of being on time. And, sure enough, no sooner had we finished our lunch than we saw LeAnn gathering children together in the middle of the plaza. We quickly took Yanna over, hugging and kissing her, trying to reassure her and trying hard to savor every last moment. We put her in line, told LeAnn and the counselors she was there, kissed her once again, and, then, in a single file line, the children all just walked away. Within a minute of when we put her in the line, she was gone. It was the most heartbreaking thing I had ever experienced.

Just before they left, LeAnn, asked if I would gather the families together and lead a prayer for the children. I agreed and a group of 50 or more of us grasped hands and prayed. We prayed for safe travel and a safe return. We prayed for the children themselves, that they would come to know the love of God and feel the warmth of his embrace. We prayed for the future and for future adoptions. And we prayed for comfort for ourselves, as we were all sad to see these children go.

Afterward, we stayed for some time, talking with the other parents and families, and just standing around. It was as if we somehow expected that, if we just waited long enough, our little girl would come back. But she did not come back, and after a while, we just went home. I don't remember much about the drive. Gone was the excitement and laughter of that trip just five weeks before. In its place was a heaviness that I can't quite describe. This wasn't just missing someone; this was as if we had lost a part of ourselves. Yanna had left thinking that she would never see us again. We knew and understood that, but we could do nothing about it. Our plans to adopt her aside, it was altogether possible that she would not be adoptable. It might well be that her biological parents still had a claim on her. It might be that she had other siblings who were also in the orphanage system and that the government would be unwilling to split them up. It could be that her records were simply lost or incomplete or that some other Russian family was interested in her and, so, would be given priority ahead of us. With all these possibilities, the likelihood was that she was not immediately available, and, so, it was very possible that she had just left our world for good. Of course, we still had our other children and our wonderful lives together. But this one special little girl, who for a season we had loved and embraced as our own, was now suddenly and perhaps permanently gone. Even now, I still hurt as I remember the pain of that afternoon. At some point on the ride home, I received a call from LeAnn, confirming that the children had boarded the plane and were safely gone. I just cried.

That night, Cricket and I sat in bed as we said our prayers together. We prayed about a lot of things, and, as we usually do, we prayed for our children. Of course, we prayed for Yanna, too. As we finished and as we lay down to sleep, Cricket said to me through her tears, "I miss Yanna." I repeated that I missed her, too, and we both just broke down and cried, as hard as either of us had ever cried. It was a sad and mournful thing, a deep hurting like I had never felt before, and hope to never experience again. It is with the greatest sympathy and respect that I say this, but I do believe I understood, even in a small way, what it felt like to lose a child. This was my daughter; it had been revealed to me ever so clearly that day in the store. The reality of it was further reinforced through the days and weeks that followed with Yanna in our family. This little girl was my daughter. I knew it, but she didn't. And I had just sent her back to Russia, perhaps never to see her again, fully well knowing that she thought she would never again see us and, perhaps, never again return.

After a long, sad weekend, I went into the office as I usually do on Monday. But I wasn't good for much; I spent most of my time sitting in my office, staring blankly out the window or looking at pictures that we had taken during Yanna's visit. At some point, I decided to write this next installment of my newsletter.

January 15, 2007

Yanna went home Friday. We went to the airport around noon. We checked her in, had lunch together, we hugged and kissed her, and then, in the blink of an eye, she was gone. It was one of the most difficult things I have ever experienced.

Afterward, a number of the families stayed behind. We held hands and prayed for the children who had just left. We lingered for some time, sharing our stories, our sorrows, and our hopes. Ultimately though, we all left with holes in our hearts.

As you know, we want to adopt Yanna, to have her as a member of our family, to live and to grow up in the love and security our home. But until that is accomplished, we ask you to continue to pray. In the short time we had her, she was such a blessing. The final week alone provided so many sweet memories. She went to church with us and signed the attendance pad. She wrote our names first, and then her name. She then wrote "Amason" after all of the names. When she realized that I saw what she had done, she quickly hid her face in embarrassment. How I long for the day when that name will be hers to keep.

Chase left for college last Saturday but came back home in time to go with us to the airport. Yanna didn't know he was coming until she saw his car in the driveway. She screamed "CHASE!" and ran and jumped into his arms. We took her to the Program's going away party. Initially, she was excited to see her friends and was reluctant to show us affection in front of them. After a while though, she began wanting us to hold her and she told a translator that she was going to stick to us "like glue" until she had to leave.

When the time came, leaving was simply hard. She asked if she could stay; she asked if we could come and get her. She told us that she loved us. All we could do was cry and promise that we loved her. We told her she was a precious and valuable child of God, with a bright and promising future. We tucked notes, cards, pictures and other small gifts into her luggage. And we told her over and over that she was special and that we would always love her. Still, when she left, she did so thinking that she would never return.

So, we are hurting, but hopeful. We look forward to the day when she returns and will truly be our daughter. I am reminded of the scripture "After you have suffered for a little while, the God of all grace, who called you to His eternal glory in Christ, will Himself perfect, confirm, strengthen, and establish you" (I Peter 5: 10). This is our prayer. We are suffering now, but that suffering cannot compare to the joy that lies ahead.

So, we thank you for your prayers and your support. You have been a blessing to us and to Yanna. And we ask that you hope and pray for the day when God confirms and establishes His plans for Yanna and for our family.

Blessings,

Allen

The Long Season

Sending Yanna back was among the saddest moments in this long saga. Indeed, it was among the saddest moments in my life. Thankfully, though, this story has a happy ending. I do have four children after all, and all four live now or grew up in our home. We were able to adopt Yanna, though it took quite a long time. During that time, we waited, we pushed and we waited some more. To this day I still question God's will and purpose in the whole thing. Why the delays? Why so long? Why did our daughter have to spend 15 more months in an orphanage 5,000 miles away when she had a family that loved her and wanted her to come home? I cannot answer any of those questions anymore now than I could at the time. I suppose it is evidence again that God moves in mysterious ways and that our role is simply to trust him and to walk in the path He sets before us. Thinking about it in that way made it easier, although it was never easy. The problem is that you are completely helpless to alter the rules of the game. And, at least in Russia, the rules are not in your favor.

Why not, some have asked? Why are the Russians not more accepting of people who are adopting children out of Russian orphanages? The children are a burden on society; so, we are saving the Russian government money and effort, right? Well, that's the typical American logic anyway; however, it's just not the way the Russians see it. Indeed, at this moment the Russian Federation has actually banned all adoptions of Russian children by U.S. citizens. Of course, the political commentators on the evening news will tell you this is in response to the *Magnitsky Act*. But let me assure you that it goes much deeper than any one bill or any one event.

So what is it? Why do Russians dislike foreign adoptions, especially by Americans, when those adoptions are, in fact, so good for the children involved? Some of it has to do with the old antagonism that was cultivated throughout the Cold War. We are the Americans, and, so, we are not to be trusted. I know that sounds like old-fashioned thinking. But those old biases and prejudices die hard and slowly. Moreover, following the collapse of the Russian economy in 1993 and the chaos that followed, many Russians blamed the Americans. As they remember it, we told them to embrace democracy and free market capitalism. Just embrace the west and become more western, we said to them through our government, our institutions and businesses. Just privatize your old state industries; open up your borders, try to imitate the America you now see on television, and everything will turn up roses. At least that is the message that many Russians heard. Well, they did all of those things, and their lives got worse. And, when they got worse, they got a whole lot worse.

Businesses and whole industries collapsed as customers exercised their newfound freedom to buy imported goods. People were out of work and could not afford their rent and property values plummeted. Wealth, whether in the form of property owned or money in the bank simply evaporated, as asset values declined and the currency was devalued. Living here in America, we got a small glimpse of what this might have been like in what we called our recent "Great Recession." Only what the Russians experienced was many times worse; it was much deeper, much more widespread and lasted much longer. Because of the diminished asset values, the old state owned industries were sold at steep discounts. The buyers of these industries were seen initially as entrepreneurs and models for the future of a new Russia; however, the image soon faded as it became apparent that these oligarchs had grown fabulously wealthy through their connections and their ability to acquire tremendously valuable resources at very low prices. Meanwhile, average Russians, who had once enjoyed a modest but comfortable existence under the old Soviet system, were now close to starving. Moreover, as the economy declined, lawlessness arose. Drug abuse, petty theft, assault, even murder, all of which were unheard of in Soviet times, became commonplace. Worse yet, organized crime moved in, filling the vacuum left by the erosion of the state and the state industries. Because of all of this, many average Russians blamed the west, and particularly the U.S., for their troubles.

So, when the administration of Vladimir Putin came to power, claiming to understand the plight of the common people, claiming to want to restore Russia to her previous greatness, and publicly blaming the U.S., its policies and culture for the problems the Russian people had experienced, his message resonated and was quickly adopted. Whereas America and Americans had been welcomed throughout the mid and late 90s, they were resented and viewed with suspicion in the mid 2000s. So, the prospect of Americans taking Russia's children away and turning them into Americans was a sore subject for many. And, amidst that negative sentiment, many Russian politicians found an opportunity.

For example, you may recall I mentioned that we were not allowed to take Yanna to see a physician. We were required to take her to the dentist and to the eye doctor, and we promised as much in writing as part of our hosting application; however, we were not allowed to take her to a general physician. In fact, if she or any of the other hosted children got sick, we were to call one of the visiting Russian physicians, provided by the hosting program. What was the logic in that? Well, there were some unscrupulous Russian politicians who had suggested that adopted children were being used for their body parts. I kid you not; in fact, it would be funny, if it were not so sad and so true. The story went something like this. Americans would host these children as a way to shop for proper donors. We would take the children to the doctor and have them checked for blood and tissue type. Then, we would adopt them, so as to harvest their body parts for the sake of our biological children and then discard whatever was left over. Now that's sick thinking, but it found fertile ground amidst some in Russia's suspicious and resentful population.

Of course, as a society, America was not without some blame. There were numerous cases of adoptions of Russian children by Americans, where the child was harmed in some way. One of the most famous of these was the terrible and sad case of Masha Allen, who was adopted and then abused by a pedophile in 1997. She was abused for five years by her adoptive father, who compounded his crime by posting elicit pictures of her on the internet. She was finally rescued by law enforcement from that terrible situation in 2003 and, in 2006, *Masha's Law* was created, establishing penalties in federal law for child pornography. Still, what Masha suffered was horrendous and unforgivable, and the Russian authorities blamed the U.S. for it. There was also the heartbreaking case of Dima Yakovlev, the toddler who died in 2008, after being left in the car in a hot parking lot in Texas. Although his father was convicted of manslaughter, some in Russia still used him as an example of the fate that awaited children adopted by Americans. In fact, the Russian law that banned adoptions by Americans was called the *Dima Yakovlev Act*. There were other cases, too, the most notorious of which was that of Artyem Saveliev, who was adopted by a woman in Tennessee, only to be sent back a few months later, alone on a plane, with a note penned inside his backpack, asking that the adoption be annulled. The mother claimed that the eight-year-old was violent and a threat to her safety. Because the authorities had not told her this, she wanted the adoption annulled. An account in the Russian press said that young Artyem had been returned, "like a pair of pants." The mother was simply unhappy with the arrangement and sent the child back, much like someone would return merchandise to a store. These cases were all true and all tragic. Some, like the case of Dima, were accidental, while others, like those of Masha and Artyem were not. Still, they all resulted in some sort of injury to the children involved, and, so, they all added fuel to that small flame of resentment, harbored by many of the Russian people.

Now, to be fair, American families have adopted more than 60,000 Russian children and the vast majority of those have gone on to live healthy and productive lives. By virtually any measure, children who are adopted are healthier and safer with brighter futures than those who are not. Indeed, no more than 1/10 of one percent of those children adopted have suffered criminal wrong doing or life threatening injury because of bad parenting. Certainly, the percentage of those who suffer harm is far greater for children who are never adopted and who grow up in Russia's decrepit orphanage system. Indeed, while reliable data are hard to come by, some have reported that the life-expectancy of "graduates" of the Russian orphanage system is barely 30 years. And that estimate is not unreasonable as these children hit the streets at the age of 17 or 18 with few marketable skills, no network of family support and a strong sense that they have little in life to lose.

Still, inside of Russia, it is more about perception than reality and, while the percentage of these few and terrible cases is very, very small, each case made the news and was exploited, either by well-intentioned but poorly informed politicians or by unscrupulous and opportunistic activists. One of such politician was a woman named Ekaterina Lakhova. An influential member of the Duma, Russia's equivalent to our House of Representatives, she was the chair of the Russian Commission on Women, Families and Demography and sponsor of the controversial *Dima Yakovlev act.* I actually met Ms. Lakhova on a business trip to Russia and was able to speak with her at length about adoption and about our daughter, Yanna. We had a pleasant conversation, although we disagreed on the basic premise of the subject.

Ms. Lakhova and many more like her, I suppose, see adoption in macro terms. Every child who leaves Russia, every child like Yanna, is not just an individual loss. Rather, they represent the loss of a larger opportunity. Yanna will not grow up in Russia; she will not have Russian children or contribute to the Russian economy. So, not only is Yanna lost to Russia and Russian society but so is what economists call the "multiplier" effect of her presence. Every impact of Yanna's life in Russia was taken away when we took her out of Russia. It's a sobering thought but it is how Ms. Lakhova saw the issue. By letting these children go, Russia was selling its future for little more than a handful of beans, for the mere savings achieved by no longer having to house, feed, clothe and educate these children. Even if keeping them was a temporary hardship, even if keeping them did

102

create emotional costs to the children, it was worth it for the sake of the larger benefit to Russia.

My response to this was simply to personalize the issue. I couldn't address the larger implications to Russian society. I couldn't promise that new children would spring up to take Yanna's place or that the economy would somehow expand, through the efforts of others, to fill the void left by Yanna's departure. I couldn't address any of that. What I could address, though, was the impact on Yanna's life and the impact on our family. Here was a dear, sweet little girl who had been abandoned by her family, who was for all practical purposes alone, and who had no one to love her as only a parent could. Moreover, here was a family who, by some miracle of God, had come to know this little girl and come to love her as our own. As I explained from the very beginning, we didn't want to adopt just any child, we wanted Yanna. To us, the issue was not and was never the impact on Russian or American society. Nothing could have been farther from our minds. This was our daughter, and she had to be with us. Imagine having one of your children taken from you; who wouldn't go to any length to bring that child home? For us, this was ever so personal and ever so real.

The contrast revealed in this conversation between Ms. Lakhova and me was eye opening. It is also emblematic of the fundamental difference between the Russian and the American viewpoints on adoption. It is this perspective that allowed Vladimir Putin to so casually dismiss evidence about the quality of life that Russian orphans have with their adopted families abroad. "So what," he retorted, "should we all just move to America then?" It is a fundamental difference of perspective that for us places the value of the individual above that of the collective. The Russians, or at least many of them, simply turn that around and put the value of the whole above that of the individual. If nothing else, my conversation with Ms. Lakhova helped me to understand that. And, because I understand it, I now feel a sense of obligation to somehow give back to Russia, for that which Russia has given me.

And So It Began

Yanna went back to Russia on January 12, 2007. With her, she took a new, pink suitcase, full of various clothes, toys, letters, pictures and other items designed to show her how much we loved her but not much else. Meanwhile, we set to work. As I mentioned earlier, Cricket had already made plans to be part of a mission team that would travel to St. Petersburg to visit, care for and love on disabled children in the orphanages designed for these special needs kids. The trip was to include a stop at Yanna's orphanage. So, Cricket and her group left for St. Petersburg on January 19, one week to the day after Yanna departed. Interestingly, this became something of a sore spot later, when the judge presiding over our adoption hearing took umbrage at Cricket's visit, along with a number of other things. Trouble though it was later, this trip was a blessing in real time. We were heart-broken over Yanna's departure and, yet, Cricket would get to see her barely two weeks after she left. I wasn't able to go, but I did see the pictures. The group took Yanna and several of her friends to an ice skating rink and to lunch at McDonald's. It was just an afternoon outing, but it was fun and it gave Cricket a chance to see our little girl, to hug her again, to fix her hair, to kiss her, tell her we loved her and to give her some more small presents that she could open on her birthday, which would be just a couple of weeks later. Of course, this short visit came to an end all too quickly, and the parting this second time was no better than it was that day in Atlanta. I learned later that Cricket cried inconsolably for an hour after having to leave Yanna again. But still, it was a visit; it was something, and it was progress. As I saw it, it was just one more step on the race that we were now running.

Meanwhile, back home, I was pinging both the hosting agency and the adoption agent that the hosting agency had recommended. We were just one of many families on the list, waiting to adopt the child we had hosted, but I wanted to make sure that we were at the top of that list. So, I called, chased, pushed, cajoled, did whatever I had to do, to move everyone else into the fast lane. By this point, we had completed every shred of paperwork that we could complete, as necessary to receive approval from the U.S. government to adopt a foreign child. And the day after Cricket left, our persistence was rewarded when the form came approving our application. This wasn't the full approval, but it was an acknowledgement that all the paperwork was in and was in order. The final step would be a digital finger-printing process, something called a biometric scan, that we would complete upon Cricket's return from St. Petersburg. I was almost smug with satisfaction at how quickly and effectively things were falling into place.

I was also learning some Russian and learning how to communicate with Yanna, despite the fact that she was so far away. Our plan was to send her a card or letter every few weeks, just to maintain our connection. In fact, it was one of those early letter-writing efforts that provided the name for this book. With Cricket going to Russia and having the chance to see Yanna in person, I thought it a good time to send her a note. I would write the letter, translate it through an online translation tool (these programs were very limited back in early 2007). I would then give it to Cricket and Cricket would give it to Yanna, who would read it and be impressed that it was written in Russian. It was a great plan, right up until the moment that I translated the Russian letter back into English. Back translation is a great way for checking accuracy. If a message that has been translated into another language is then back-translated into the original language and if the message is largely unchanged, the quality of the translation is judged to be pretty good.

In this instance, the quality of the translation was apparently not very good. My letter had begun, "Dear Yanna," which is customary in English. Once translated into Russian though, the letter read "Expensive Yanna," which was not the intent. I remember telling Olga about this just before the mission team departed for Russia. She just laughed at the translation. Apparently the Russians do not use the word "Dear" as we do in letter greetings. Thus, the translation program did not know how to handle this word other than to assume I had meant to say "precious" or "expensive." It was funny but it served as a metaphor for the process. Yanna was dear to us and the process of adoption was quite expensive; however, it was also a study in misunderstanding, in cultural relativity and difference, and in the difficulty trying to do something well, when that thing itself is so fundamentally unfamiliar.

So, Cricket returned from her trip to Russia on January 28 and, on February 7 we traveled yet again to Atlanta, this time to a completely charmless USCIS facility in a warehouse off of I-75, where we sat and waited for our names to be called. We then learned that the biometric scan amounted to having our finger and handprints scanned into what looked like a fancy copy machine. The process itself took no more than five minutes, and we were done. Then, no more than two weeks later, we received the approved and official form, I-600. In fact, I still have the form. I kept a file, documenting each step in the process. And, given all the work it took to put this all together, I made copies of everything and then I made copies of copies. At this point, Yanna had been back in Russia for five weeks, and here we sat, ready to petition the Russia government to make us her parents.

So, pause with me for a minute and let's think about where we are in this story. Our daughter, Yanna, is back in Russia. It's late in February of 2007, and we are ready to go, ready to put together something called a dossier, which would be submitted to the Russian government. To say we had moved quickly would be like saying that Luciano Pavarotti was just some singer. We had moved with record speed to this point, and I saw no reason to slow down. Of course, there was still one essential piece missing from the overall puzzle. We had never met our adoption agent, nor had we ever spoken with him for more than two minutes over the phone. Yet, without him, we were going nowhere fast.

Justin was his name. He was the owner and chief operative of a company called Children of the World Adoptions, based in New York. He was a Romanian-born, Russian-educated attorney, with licenses to practice law in both the U.S. and Russia. He was also a registered adoption agent in Russia, and, so, was able to submit dossiers to the Russian government, on behalf of adopting families, like us. He was also paranoid, abrupt, dismissive and completely unable to listen to anything beyond his own suspicions and opinions. Oh, and his accent was so thick that he was barely understandable. All that aside, though, he was also the best, I mean the absolute best. To this day, Justin is also my friend. In fact, I spoke with him as recently as January of 2013. We just keep in touch; I'll do him any favor he asks, and my family and I have a standing invitation to visit him should we ever be in his area.

Well, Justin had one way of doing things, his way. And, even though I had all of the documents, all of the paperwork, including the I-600, there was one very important thing that had not yet been done. We had not yet determined if Yanna was adoptable. Recall that many of the hosted children cannot be adopted. It may be that they have families who have not relinquished their rights yet. It might be that they have siblings in the orphanage system, or that they simply do not want to leave Russia. Even in the mid 2000s, the Russian system gave every benefit of the doubt to the children or to Russian citizens who might have had a claim on them. Given this, it was completely possible that Yanna was not adoptable and that we had done all of this work for nothing. Now, we had heard from the hosting agency director, and from Lydia, the orphanage director, that they both thought Yanna was adoptable. So, we were optimistic; however, the final word on this belonged to Justin.

Why was his judgment so special? Well, because as a registered adoption agent in Russia, he had access to a secure government database with the adoption status of all the registered orphans. If Yanna was in the database, and if she had been in the database for six months, she could be adopted by foreign parents, like us. If she was in the database, but, if she had not been there for at least six months, then we would have to wait. The reason for this was to give Russian citizens the first opportunity to adopt these Russian orphans. For the first six months the children are in the database, they are available to any Russian family but unavailable to foreigners.

So, it would be disappointing to find Yanna had not crossed this important threshold. But it would only slow us down; it wouldn't change the overall plan. The bigger fear was that Yanna might not be in the database at all. Plain and simple, if she wasn't in the database, then she wasn't available, end of story.

That would be heartbreaking and it happened all too often. Sometimes for legitimate reasons; a parent was ill, so the child was placed in an orphanage. But there is no crime in being ill, and the government would never take children away from parents who might, one day, recover. But there were other reasons that children might not be in the database. It might simply be a matter of bureaucratic tomfoolery, the wrong form in the wrong stack, such that the child never got entered in. Sometimes, though, the issue was more sinister. Some orphanage directors wouldn't put the children into the database unless they were paid a bribe by an adoption agent or a family, perhaps. Still others were just lazy, uncaring or, for some reason, opposed to adoption. So, it was possible that Yanna would be like many other children, available for adoption as a matter of fact, but not in the database and so unavailable as a matter of law. It was a significant risk and a frightening prospect.

The way Justin chose to handle this was to have a single meeting, in Atlanta, with all the parents who had hosted children and were now seeking to adopt. Of that group of 20 or so families, we were the farthest along. All we needed was the good word from Justin, and we would begin packing. So, we traveled to Atlanta, yet again, for this meeting. After some long, and largely unnecessary explanations about the process from Phyllis, Justin's wife, our turn came to sit down for the one-on-one meeting. I say unnecessary only because we had already done everything. We had our I-600 in hand, while many of the families in the room were still casting about for a home study. So, as important as the information that Phyllis provided was, it wasn't the reason we were there. We needed to hear one word, "adoptable," and, with that, we would be off, like the down on a thistle. So, we sat down with Justin, a man in his 70's, with a Russian / Romanian accent as thick as peanut butter. He takes a scrap of paper from his pocket, reads Yanna's full Russian name and says, "yes," she is in the database and has been there for more than six months! Yes!! We could start the process, and Yanna would soon be ours!

That was at least the way I saw it. I would soon come to find out that it wasn't quite that simple. You see, just because we are ready to submit a dossier, doesn't mean that the Russian government is ready to accept it. In fact, the government department that handled adoptions had decided that, in St. Petersburg, they would handle only about 12 dossiers per month. And, of those 12, they had also decided that two could come from Children of the World, Justin's agency. Why 12 and why two? Gosh, who knows... you might as well ask why it always seems to rain on the weekends. The government could just arbitrarily decide to only accept only six dossiers per month. So, there was no point in asking; you might end up irritating them and make things worse. For us, what it meant was that, even though we were ready, we could not submit until our turn came up in Justin's queue. And we were still a month or two away from that.

The Time Had Come

As hard as it was to wait a month or two, it was a small hurdle. We now knew Justin; we knew that he could get us the result that we wanted. We knew that Yanna was available for adoption, and we knew that we had our I-600. So we would submit in March instead of February. We would still have Yanna home before the end of the school year, no more than three months since that heart-breaking day at the airport. All in all, life was still good, and we were still on track.

It seemed to us then the time had come to tell Yanna of our plans. Remember, we could not mention adoption during the hosting process. And this made perfect sense to us, as it was completely possible that there would be no adoption. The child might not be in the database. The family might not qualify for the I-600 or be able to pay the fees and other costs required by the adoption agent and by the process in general. So, the rule was, you did not use the "A" word. As hard as it was, we had followed that rule, using words like "project platypus" in place of adoption and being sure never to suggest directly to Yanna what was coming. That's part of why sending her back was so hard. We had hoped that we would soon be her forever family, but we knew that she had no idea about this. She went back to her orphanage, thinking that it was and would be her home for a very long time.

Of course, understanding this all as we did, we often wondered about the timing and setting of the big reveal. Who would tell Yanna and how? What would her reaction be? What sorts of questions would she have, and who would be there to answer her questions? It was a huge deal, and we had no idea as to how it was going to work. So, as I often do when faced with an uncertainty, I decided that we should just take matters into our own hands. We would tell Yanna about the adoption and we would do it in person. What is more, because Cricket had been to St. Petersburg just a few weeks earlier, the honor would fall to me. I would travel to Russia; I would visit Yanna in her orphanage, and I would tell her that she was our daughter. And, so, the planning for the trip began, and my excitement began to build.

The first thing I needed was a story, a reason to visit St. Petersburg that would make the visa application easier and that would allow me to offset some of the expense. As a professor, that part of the plan was easy enough. I searched online for universities in or around St. Petersburg where I might be invited to lecture, to collaborate on some research or to teach a class. I didn't need them to pay me; I simply needed them to invite me. My university provided generous travel and support for scholars on legitimate academic business. So, what I needed was some legitimate academic business in Russia.

Three schools responded to my request and were interested in having me come to lecture or speak. One of those was a small, Christian university, with a small, residential campus just east of the city centre. As it turns out, this university, St. Petersburg Christian University (SPCU), had provided the space that housed Cricket's mission team just a few weeks earlier. The Rector of SPCU was a man, about my age, named Alexander Negrov. Alexander was born Ukrainian, and like all Ukranians of his generation, had grown up in the Soviet Union. He had gone to university, studied engineering and done a mandatory stint in the Soviet army as an artillery officer. As an adult, he had come to know Jesus, studied at seminary and committed himself to full-time ministry. When the Soviet Union collapsed, many of the former states reverted to their original status as independent countries. Ukraine then ceased to be a part of the larger U.S.S. R. Alexander became a foreigner in what was once his own country.

This is one of the more fascinating human realities that I came to appreciate during this long process. The Soviet Union was more than just a country. As I discussed earlier, in the U.S. we saw the U.S.S.R. as our adversary, a red monolith, like that front wall of the Kremlin that faces Red Square. We never understood that it was a collection of states; all of which once held independent status; all of which had a unique people and identity and many of which longed for independence. Well, Alexander knew he was Ukranian, of course. But all he ever knew was Ukraine as a part of the

Soviet Union. He grew up speaking Russian, and, as a part of the Soviet military, he traveled across what seemed one enormous country. So, when he learned that he would have to declare his citizenship, either as a Ukranian, or as a Russian, he was a bit perplexed. He was from Ukraine and that is where his parents still lived. But he had no idea that in claiming to be Ukrainian, he would lose the ability to enter and exit Russia as he pleased and to use its facilities and services as he once did. I remember feeling so sorry for him, as he explained all this to me. Yes, it was great that we in the west "won" the Cold War, but we should understand that the fall of the Soviet Union created a tremendous hardship for millions upon millions of people who had no connection whatsoever to communism, the government or the crimes of the past. Alexander was one of those people.

But I'm getting ahead of myself. Before I knew any of this, I simply knew Alexander as a contact and a potential colleague. I had sent him a random email, explaining that I was a U.S. professor, specializing in international strategic management. I explained that I had interests in Russia and that I would be traveling there soon and so was looking for opportunities to connect with local universities. Alexander responded with interest. As a Christian university, in a country that had once been hostile to Christianity, SPCU had worked to build a reputation in areas of more general, secular interest. One such area was that of leadership. As Alexander explained it to me, Russian society needed a new generation of leaders. For decades, people had been told what to do by the government. They had little autonomy and little choice about their own lives and virtually no sense of leading and directing others. Thus, the new Russia, with all of its emerging businesses, institutions, opportunities and practices, needed good, honest leaders. And at least some of the training for that emerging class of leaders could come from SPCU. I still credit my friend Alexander for his vision in understanding the need and in trying to find a way to address it.

Well, given this, he saw me as an opportunity, an America professor, with specific expertise in organizational leadership and strategy, who was also a Christian, and able to fund his own travel to St. Petersburg. Once, again, it seemed like a match made in heaven; SPCU needed me and I needed it. So, we settled on a topic and a format; I would deliver three evening lectures on various elements of leadership. We set a date, and the planning began. SPCU marketed my lectures to its student body and throughout its community of contacts. Its staff sent me an LOI, or letter of invitation, and I began applying for my Russian entry visa. I bought my airline tickets, communicated with Mike the missionary about my plans, timing and agenda, and I reached out to the person who would be my translator, driver and guide, Sasha.

Who was Sasha? Wow, what a question. To answer it, let me start in the here and now; Sasha is a close family friend. She is the wife of a man from Texas, named Tuner. She is the mother of a sweet little boy named Alexander (although, for reasons unrelated to this story, I call him "W").

She lives in Connecticut but works for an NGO based in Washington, that works to promote healthy Russian families. She is a beautiful woman, inside and out, and one of the few people in this world who could ask and expect to receive anything from me that I could possibly give. The history that we share, Sasha and our family, binds us in a way that is rare even within families but that is almost unheard of outside of families. Perhaps that is why I took to calling her "aunt" Sasha to Yanna and our other children and why I would introduce her as my sister on many occasions over the years that followed. Sasha is more than just a close friend; she's just Sasha, the one and only.

Of course, she is all of that now. Back in March of 2007, I barely knew her. She was just a local Russian, a Christian translator for a number of organizations, including Mike's ministry. And that's how we first met. Sasha had been the translator, logistics manager, and on the ground supervisor for several missions teams sent from our church in Athens to St. Petersburg. So, on one of Mike's visits home, Sasha had come along to meet and be met by the members of the church and, interestingly enough, to look at a graduate program at my university, The University of Georgia. So, I knew who Sasha was; she and I had even had a brief conversation once. She had also been the coordinator and translator for the mission team that Cricket had traveled with just weeks before. So, I sent Sasha a note, explained to her about my upcoming visit and the purpose for it and asking if she would arrange my transportation, be my translator and just generally babysit and keep me out of trouble for the three days that I would be in Russia. It was a business arrangement; I would pay her and she would take care of me. At least that's the way I presented it. She agreed, graciously, and so began our connection and friendship.

I left for Russia on Sunday, April 8 with plans to return on Thursday, April 12. It was a short visit, but it was well scripted and would afford me all the time I needed to do all I needed to do. There were three somewhat independent parts to the agenda. First, I would do a good job for SPCU and Alexander. I had prepared my materials and sent them ahead to be translated, and I had read up on business and society in Russia. I would meet with Mike and his wife Olga. This too was a growing friendship. I knew of Mike and Olga, of course. And during the actual hosting program, had interacted with them on a number of occasions. But I had never visited them, shared a meal with them or really spent much time getting to know them. So, I was looking forward to that. Finally, I would also spend as much time as possible with Yanna, and, when the time was right, I would tell her about our plans.

The flight over was long, with a stop in Paris, where I caught the second leg of my journey to St. Petersburg. For those who have never been to Charles de Gualle Airport in Paris, let me explain that it's like a trip through the U.N. but with more luggage. It is among the world's larger and busier airports, and people from all over the world pass through there. In the process of changing planes, you can expect to spend time on multiple buses and in multiple terminal buildings, and you can expect to hear languages ranging from French to English to Spanish to Arabic to Russian. Yes, I heard Russian speakers on the bus that took us out to our plane. Now, there is really not much about that that is surprising. After all, I was boarding a plane for St. Petersburg, Russia, and, at least half of those on the flight with me were Russians, returning home. But I was particularly aware of it and filled with both fascination and trepidation. Would I ever meet any of these Russians in the process of the adoption? Perhaps, one of them worked for the court or for the committee that administered the orphanages. What would these Russians think if they knew why I was visiting their country? Would they think anything about it at all? I had spent very little time around people from Russia; until just a few months prior, I had never had any real reason or interest.

I touched down in St. Petersburg in the late afternoon, tired but none the worse for wear. I sailed through customs and passport control. I even tried to speak to the passport agent in her own language. She was not particularly impressed but did manage the faintest hint of a smile, or perhaps a laugh, at my poor pronunciation. Mike met me in the arrivals hall; we collected our things and set out. St. Petersburg is a beautiful city but also an austere and intimidating one. To me, it was surreal to see the monuments to the Red Army, to the victory in the Great Patriotic War (what we call World War II), and to the terrible siege of

Leningrad. I won't tell that whole story but, for those who don't know, the Nazis had invaded Russia during the war. While St. Petersburg, which was called Leningrad at the time, offered little of strategic value to the Nazis, it was still an important city and so would provide an important symbolic victory. But, rather than risk men and ammunition attacking it, the invaders decided to simply encircle it and starve its people with a blockade. This siege lasted nearly 18 months, during which time nearly one million of the city's residents died. The airport in St. Petersburg is named Pulkova Airport and is within sight of the Pulkova heights, a ridge of small hills or mountains, where the Nazis established their southern line.

I knew this history and saw these monuments. I knew the communists had used propaganda related to the war to promote patriotism and paranoia of the outside world. I also knew that the Soviets were guilty of enormous atrocities themselves but glossed over them in describing their great victory. So, in seeing all of this, I was fascinated and more than a little conflicted. I saw an enormous statue of Lenin on a public square and, of course, I saw rampant commercialism on display with shops, advertising, and cars and shoppers everywhere. It was a fascinating and exciting experience. Mike and Olga took me to their home, a beautiful flat on the top floor of an old building, very near the center of the city. Mike explained that, during communist times, two families had shared this one small apartment. We had tea together, and I unpacked those things that I had brought over for Mike and his ministry. After which, we went to dinner, Chinese of course. What else would an American eat in Russia? We then went to SPCU, where Mike and Olga helped me check in at the front desk and get settled in the residence.

The residence was a small, one bedroom apartment, with a separate kitchen and bathroom. There were clean linens, a firm but comfortable bed, a table and chairs, and a sofa. There was even food in the refrigerator and coffee on the counter. Someone had gone to great lengths to make certain that I was comfortable and well provided for. So, I stretched out on the bed, and fell fast asleep. I woke the next morning and decided to explore a bit. So, I walked out of the gated campus and wandered around the neighborhood. I was later told that this was a very dangerous thing for an American to do. Oh, well, thankfully it turned out all right. I even found a McDonald's, where I bought a muffin and a cup of coffee. When I returned, I went to the front office and was introduced to Alexander. He and I sat and talked for about an hour before Sasha arrived to pick me up.

Sasha had planned our itinerary carefully. We would take a bus to a car rental facility, where I would rent a car, that she would drive. So, the two of us rode around town together quite a bit. In fact, on that first day and on that first trip, I learned that Sasha and I already shared some history. Recall that Cricket had been part of a mission team in St. Petersburg, just a few weeks before and that Sasha had been the facilitator and manager for that team. So, they had spent a lot of time together. What is more, the team had arranged for each person to lead a brief devotional each day. Well, when Cricket's turn came, her devotion was on how God can change the heart. To illustrate her point, she took copies of my newsletters and read them to the team. I had never really thought about it before, but the letters did illustrate a progression of the heart. Remember, I wrote these letters over the course of several weeks and mostly as a way to simply keep people informed. I didn't anticipate or plan any spiritual structure or meaning. But, now that they were done, if you read them first to last in quick succession, you could certainly see the shift in tone and message and so see how God was changing my heart. Well, this was Cricket's devotion, and it touched Sasha in a particular and personal way.

When she explained this to me, I was surprised and a little embarrassed, but it gave me the opportunity to begin talking with Sasha about her life, family and dreams. It accelerated our relationship, beyond just the business arrangement that I had envisioned to something more. Like Christian siblings, we were able to share about our experiences and hopes for the future. We talked about communism and her life before the fall of the Soviet Union. We talked about her mother, father and sister. We talked about our children and our plans for adopting Yanna. We talked about her volunteer work in the orphanages and with Mike and his ministry, and we talked about Cricket's heart for Russia and the seed that was planted all those many years ago. We talked as we rode along together, sharing with such intensity that I barely noticed when she turned down an alley and through a gate, coming to a stop in front of an industrial looking, three-story brick building in an area north of the city, crowded with large apartment blocks, separated by a network of single lane streets, choked with dumpsters and parked cars. Where are we, I asked? Sasha looked surprised by my question and answered, "This is Yanna's orphanage." My heart skipped a beat; after all these months and miles, I was here.

We walked in through the double doors, the same doors through which Yanna would have walked out when she came to visit us. I was introduced to the guard, a traditional and stereotypically thick and gruff man of, perhaps, 50. After a short wait in the lobby, Lydia, the orphanage director came out to greet me. She was thrilled to see me again and ushered Sasha and me into her office, where tea and cake awaited. We were joined soon thereafter by another woman named Valentina, who was the education director at the orphanage. Valentina clearly had a heart for the children and she asked me straight away, "have you completed your home study yet?" I was shocked; this was a secret, right? Well, apparently not any more, and at least not in this circle of friends.

So, I filled them both in on the progress we had made and on our timeline. They both approved and offered various words of advice. They also asked about our other children, about Cricket and about our plans for Yanna's school and life in America. At some point, during this casual conversation, there was a knock at the door. Lydia said something to the effect of come in, and through the door burst my baby girl! She smiled broadly as she ran across the room and jumped into my arms. I could have held her forever. Sasha and Lydia talked for a bit, mostly about the logistics of my visit. Sasha had arranged to be allowed to take Yanna out of the orphanage. This was more than I had imagined possible, and, so, I was very excited, of course. As I was not a Russian citizen, I really had no business even being there, and this would be a sticking point later. Still, Sasha could take Yanna out for the day with Lydia's approval. It just so happened that on this particular day, I would be with them.

It was already late in the day, and I was to give the first of my three lectures that evening. So, we left the orphanage and drove back to SPCU, where we took a walk in a nearby park and went for a late lunch at McDonald's. It was on our walk that I learned from Yanna that she had once lived in this neighborhood. In the period of time after she was taken from her biological parents but before she was placed in her orphanage, she had lived with a foster family in this very neighborhood. Learning this made me a bit nervous. Recall that Russians were given preference and could adopt a Russian child ahead of any foreigner. I did not want Yanna's former foster family seeing her, recognizing her and deciding that they wanted her back. Sasha convinced me that I was being paranoid. Still, there are worse things than a healthy bit of caution and the mere fact that I was paranoid didn't mean that there was nothing to fear.

I won't bore you with the details of my lecture that night, but it went very well, and Alexander was very pleased. The crowd was likely about 50 – 60 people, made up half and half students and people from the community. Sasha and Yanna came and sat in the back. Mike was also there, along Olga and two women from the staff of his charity, Masha O. and Masha M. They all at least pretended to be interested in the topic. One funny story I will share from this event came at the very beginning. I mentioned earlier that I had developed a presentation that someone on Alexander's staff had translated into Russian. The first slide of that presentation had the title of my talk, along with my name and position. Well, apparently the translator had some difficulty with the name Amason. After all, how do you translate a proper noun into a language with a completely different alphabet? Apparently they had simply transliterated it, substituting the Russian letters most similar, in their judgment, to the letters and sounds in English. Well, whatever they did, Yanna did not like the result and she protested out loud at seeing her future name spelled in a way other than she had been spelling it. Funny stuff.

After the talk, the group of us, including Mike, Olga, the two Mashas, Sasha, Yanna and I went out to dinner. We went to a place like a Café Uno, a European pizza and Italian eatery. It may well have been Café Uno, for all I recall. What ever it was, it was good and it was fun. While we were there, Yanna told Sasha in Russian that this was the first time, other than during her time in America, she had been to a restaurant with table service. Now, that in and of itself isn't particularly noteworthy. By definition, anyone who has ever been to a restaurant, had to go for the very first time, at some point. And many, many people around the world have never been to any restaurant at all, table serving or otherwise. What made this noteworthy was that Yanna told Sasha but also asked her not to tell me. Did she imagine that I thought she was a debutante? Was she embarrassed for me to know that she did not live like an upper-middle class American? Did she fear I would love her less because she had not enjoyed all the things that I had been blessed to enjoy? The irony is that I was prepared to give it all away, to spend everything we had if necessary to get her. Heck, I was excited that she got to enjoy her first trip to a real restaurant with her new, real father.

To paraphrase an old Jim Croce song, though, isn't that the way it always goes in our relationship with our Heavenly Father too? All He wants is for us to be with Him. Yet, we're embarrassed; we with think we're not good enough or that, if He really sees us as we truly are, that He'll somehow love us less. And, so, we keep our distance. We confide in our friends, and we look for our own solutions. Yet, all the time, He is standing right there, just happy to be out with us, happy to pick up the check and happy that we are with Him, rather than with someone else. For me at least, this was one of several watershed moments in this whole long saga. Yanna liked us, and she liked being with us. But she did not yet fully trust us nor did she trust what was happening to the course of her life. And that pattern is true of all of us. As God rescues us and brings us out of one life and into another, our fear, shame or simple inability to understand it all holds us back and keeps us from entering into the full and new life before us. Having seen this little exchange and having thought about it, I knew the time was right.

So, after dinner, Sasha, Yanna and I said goodbye to the group and made our way down the street for some ice cream. And it was at this little ice cream shop, that Sasha read to Yanna a letter that Cricket and I had written to her. The text of the letter is actually quite personal; so I am not going to copy it. But what it said was that we loved her, pretty much from the moment we first saw her. It explained that we were already well along in the process to adopt her. And it explained that our plan was for her to come into our family and grow up in our home, with us as her real parents.

By the time this had all transpired, it was getting late, and we needed to get Yanna back. In fact, we were later than we had told the orphanage staff we were going to be, and they were a bit upset when we returned. I felt badly about that. Lydia and the staff were very supportive and proved invaluable allies throughout the whole process. The last thing I wanted to do was to violate their trust or compromise their good work. So, we promised that it wouldn't happen again. I kissed Yanna goodbye and we left.

The next two days were very much like the first one. I would get up, have coffee and an hour or so of discussion with Alexander. Sasha would come and collect me sometime in the mid-morning. We would drive up to the orphanage, get Yanna and then set out on some adventure. At the end of the day, I would give my lecture, and we would take Yanna back. On the second day, Sasha and I were allowed to take Yanna into the city center, where she was to receive an award for a picture she had drawn. Afterward, we walked around and saw some of the sights of the city. It was cold and, as we walked, Yanna liked either for me to carry her or to hold her hand. Sasha, often took pictures of us, sometimes with our knowledge, sometimes not. But it was on this day and during a walk through the city that Sasha snapped the picture that is on the front of this book. I still remember the setting clearly and remember holding on to Yanna, as we walked along the sidewalk. I reflected on the night before and on the conversation at the restaurant. She might not fully understand just what it meant to have a real father, who would love her, protect and provide for her, but that is what she had. And now that I had her, I wasn't letting go.

We Hit the Wall

Like Cricket weeks before, I cried after dropping Yanna off for the final time. Sasha took me back to my apartment at the university where I packed and prepared for the trip home, but I slept poorly that night and, by the time I left for the airport in the morning, I was a wreck, completely exhausted, physically and emotionally. So, I slept a bit on the plane, which is out of character for me, and felt better by the time I arrived back in Atlanta. I perked up even more on the drive from the airport back home when I received a call from Justin. In fact, I had just pulled out of the airport and onto the expressway when the phone range. It was my Romanian adoption agent extraordinaire and he was calling with good news. "Allen," he said through his thick accent, "we are just about ready to begin working on your dossier. Do you have everything ready? Phyllis will call you later this week and tell you what to do." And there it was, the final step. We'd put our dossier together in record time; we'd submit it at the first opportunity, and I would be back in Russia before the end of the next month. To borrow another famous phrase from the world of entertainment, I love it when a plan comes together.

It was April 12 in the afternoon, as I drove home satisfied and smug, from my trip to St. St. Petersburg. Having been away for a week, Friday was full of work. I was a department chair and my university was among the more bureaucratic organizations anywhere in the world. So, there was plenty of work to occupy my time and attention. Besides, until Phyllis called, I wouldn't know what to work on anyway. So, for that day and the several that followed, life returned to normal. When Phyllis did call, sometime in the middle of the next week, she had predictable news. It was time to put together our Russian dossier, which meant taking everything that we had done already and getting it into a new and different format. It also meant getting some other documents that were required by the Russians but not required in the U.S.

For example, the Russian government requires that adopting families certify that the sewage systems in their homes can accommodate an extra occupant. Now, on one level, I can see that; our family did go from five to six people and it wasn't like the newest member was an infant. So, they wanted to make sure that our sewage system could handle the load. But on another level, think about that for a minute. Just how was I supposed to certify that our house, which has a septic system, was sufficient? I mean, it's not like the request came with instructions. So, I called a plumber, explained the situation and asked him to come take a look and write a letter "certifying" that our septic system was sufficient to handle six people. That letter, like many others just like it, was then signed, counter-signed, notarized, apostilled, and added to the file.

But I'm getting ahead of myself again. For now, let's just agree that the process was detailed, thorough and, occasionally, downright bewildering. Still, each step brought Yanna a little closer to home. So, our attitude was, just do it. Like digging a ditch, each form, each letter, each document, each signature and certification were just another shovel full of dirt. You dug in, you scooped it up and then you threw it aside. That was my mindset as I listened to Phyllis describe what was needed. Rather than focus on the whole, on that enormous mountain of stuff that needed to be moved, I focused instead on just the next shovel and what had to happen to move it aside. There was a lot to do, but it was all doable, all it took was effort and perseverance.

As it turned out, though, sometimes even effort and perseverance aren't enough. You can plan, work, anticipate, adapt and work some more. And everything can go just right or even better than just right, right up until that moment when it all goes wrong. And that is what happened here. No more than a week after I returned from Russia, barely three days after my talk with Phyllis regarding the preparation of our dossier, I received a call from Justin. "Allen," he said, "I have some bad news." My heart sank; what could have happened? I mean, we had done everything right. We were ready to prepare the final dossier; what could possibly go wrong now?

To understand what had gone wrong, you need to understand a little about the formal structure of the adoption machinery in Russia. Recall that Children of the World was an adoption agency with official accreditation from the Russian government. The official accreditation is much like a license to do business. As the chief executive of an accredited agency, Justin could access that database that I discussed earlier. He could get information on the children and, most importantly, he had standing before the Russian government and in the court system. So, he could file the paperwork petitioning for an adoption, and he could represent clients in the adoption proceedings. So accreditation was essential. Without it, you couldn't start the adoption process; you couldn't even get in the front door. Another sad reality we came to appreciate is that many prospective adoptive parents learn about this the hard way.

Taken in by the sales pitch of an unscrupulous adoption agency or persuaded by bad advice, some parents have hired adoption agents who, though licensed to work in the U.S. or China, Latvia or some other country, are not accredited in Russia. So, these poor parents might put together paperwork, get a home study completed, along with their biometric scans and their I-600s, only to find out that their agent was not recognized by the Russian government.

Thankfully, that was not our problem; Justin and his agency were fully accredited and well known in Russia, and in St. Petersburg in particular. But like all accredited agencies, his accreditation was temporary and needed to be renewed annually. For Children of the World, the reaccreditation cycle occurred in March. Justin filed the application for reaccreditation in January; however, January, then February then March came and went, with no action taken on his application. At the end of the month, March 2007, the Russian government informed him, through his employee in Moscow, that no agencies were being reaccredited in 2007, until a complete review of the accreditation process was undertaken. Why was this? What was the point of such a review?

Recall that many forces within Russia opposed foreign adoption in general. There was also the steady drumbeat in the Russian media that adopted children were often abused and that adoption agencies were facilitating the sale of Russian children for no reason other than their own profit. And, sometimes, though very infrequently, some adoption agencies did in fact break the rules. One such rule calls for a series of post-placement reports. The Russian government insisted that these reports be filed at the three month, six month, one year and two year mark following the adoption. The point was simply to check on the child, to determine his or her welfare and to see how he or she was doing in the new family. Of course, once a child is adopted and living in the U.S., the Russian government has no way to enforce this part of the bargain. Parents could simply, and selfishly, refuse to comply, refuse to spend the money for these home studies and refuse to have their post-placement reports completed and sent. So, the Russian government required that the agencies provide the reports. If the agencies did not comply, then they ran the risk of losing their accreditation.

Children of the World handled this problem with a contract. As part of the contract for services, we agreed to hire a licensed social worker to complete the series of post placement visits and reports and to send those reports back to Russia through Children of the World in the proper format and at the proper time. Failing to fulfill our end of this contract meant that we could be liable to Children of the World for significant monetary damages. So, we took this requirement seriously because our adoption agency took it seriously, but not every agency was equally committed – especially agencies that were inexperienced or that had decided to quit doing business in Russia. These would often just walk away from their obligation to provide post placement reporting. That sort of thing, combined with a few well-publicized, and sometimes over-sensationalized, stories of heartbreak or abuse was enough to convince the Russian bureaucracy that a complete review of the whole accreditation process was in order. Let me underscore as well that this wasn't an effort to extort. Despite popular notions to the contrary, this wasn't about money at all. There was no favoritism, bribery or corruption in this process. No agencies were being reaccredited, regardless of their connections or their past performance. This was to be a complete review.

How long would a complete review take? Maybe a few weeks, a few months, perhaps a year or more, at the time, there was just no way to know. All we knew was that the process had suddenly stopped. Without his license in effect, Justin could not submit any dossiers to the Russian government. And it just so happened that our dossier was next, right there at the top of his pile. Yanna was still in an orphanage 5,000 miles away, and our dossier was finished and ready to go. Nevertheless, the machinery had simply stopped. No applications were accepted, and no new adoptions could begin. So, until this review was completed, and until Children of the World was reaccredited, we were suddenly at a complete and utter standstill.

And so, I as often did throughout this process, I took out my trusty laptop and wrote another installment of my newsletter to those who were following this saga.

April, 23 2007

*When I last wrote to you, Yanna had just returned
to Russia and we were just beginning the adoption
process. That was nearly 4 months ago. Since
then, a lot has happened and I wanted to catch you
up. I also wanted to enlist your continued
support. As you prayed for Yanna and for us
during her visit, I ask that you continue to pray
now. Our little girl is not yet home and our family
is not yet whole. We love Yanna dearly and
believe in our hearts that she is already our
daughter. So, we ask that you continue to pray for
God's deliverance and restoration.*

*First, to update you on the process; we are getting
closer. We have the approval of the U.S.
government and we know that Yanna is cleared
and available for adoption. Those are two big
hurdles and we give thanks and praise to have
cleared them. So, we are ready to submit our
application. However, the Russian government is
not accepting applications right now. Indeed, at
present there are no adoption agencies licensed to
submit international applications in Russia. The
Russian government has not renewed any licenses
for 2007 and so will not accept any new
applications. Our attorney tells us that this has
happened before and that, in time, the process will
open up again. When it does, we'll be ready. But,
until then, we no choice but to wait.*

*The good news is that we have been to see Yanna.
In January, Cricket went to St. Petersburg as a
part of a mission team. While there, the team
visited Yanna's orphanage and got to take her and
several of her friends out for some ice skating and
lunch. It was just an afternoon but it was a great
time. Cricket got see Yanna and to talk with her;*

she even got to fix Yanna's hair. As you can imagine though, saying good bye was hard.

I visited as well, just a few weeks ago and I was able to take Yanna out each of the three days I was in town. We had a wonderful time together. We went shopping and ice skating; we went out for lunch and dinner. We even got to go to a ceremony where Yanna received an award for a picture she had drawn. While it was special for me, it must have been especially so for her. You see, the day before, I told Yanna of our plans to adopt her. I simply told her everything that was on my heart, that we loved her and wanted to be her real parents. That our family was not complete without her; that she had a new sister and brothers who were waiting to welcome her home. Mostly, though, I reassured her of her value and importance and I told her that, even when she was old, she would always be our little girl. It was a very special moment and one that I will never forget.

But, as good as it was, it still came to an abrupt end. I took Yanna back to her orphanage and I prayed over her. I told her to be strong and patient, to never doubt our love and to rest assured that we thought about and prayed for her every single day. I told her that we would work everyday to bring her home and I told her that we would be back as soon as we could. She hugged me one final time and then I left.

So, that is where we are. We speak with her every couple of weeks, for just a few minutes. We also send her cards and letters, every week or two. Just so that she knows she hasn't been forgotten. Our dear friend Sasha goes by periodically and takes her out for the day. Sasha sends us pictures

*and reassures us that all is well. And really, she's
right. God is good and God is in control. We are
just waiting for His deliverance. In the meantime,
He is showing us that His grace is sufficient for us
and for Yanna. Since the day she left us I have
clung to a verse of scripture that says "After you
have suffered for a little while, the God of all
grace, who called you to His eternal glory in
Christ, will Himself perfect, confirm, strengthen,
and establish you" (I Peter 5: 10). We are
confident that God has called us to this. He
brought Yanna into our lives and He moved us to
fall so completely in love with her. As with our
other children, we believe that God has given
Yanna to us as gift, and we are blessed to have
her.*

*So, we ask you to pray with us, to agree with us,
and to wait with us, for God to perfect and confirm
His gift and to strengthen and establish our family
by bringing Yanna home soon. You all have been
a great blessing to us and we thank God for you.*

Blessings,

Allen

Time and Testing

Time is a funny thing. In many ways, time is
paradoxical and can be understood in one way, while in fact
being something entirely different. Think about this for a
moment if you will; we certainly know that each day, like
ever other day is 24 hours long. Each hour consists of 60
minutes, and each minute consists of 60 seconds. And every
second is exactly like all the others. So, in a very real sense,
time is linear. No second, minute or hour is any longer than

any of the others; each hour and day pass at the rate of all those that have gone before. One hour is exactly 1/24th of a day and each day is but a small fraction of each week, month and year. But, even while we know this is true, it never really seems so. While we can know that time is linear and even in the pace of its passing, it can still seem completely non-linear and uneven. There are times when time just seems to fly, and there are times when it seems frozen in place. Sitting on a long flight or lying awake in bed, you can experience minutes that seem to last for hours. In the same way, enjoying a night out with your sweetheart or day on the lake with your children, and time will disappear like smoke in the wind. When you are waiting for Christmas, your birthday or for the start of a vacation, the calendar will slow to a crawl and days will seem like weeks. Yet, once these days are gone and the thrill of the expectation is passed, time seems to accelerate back into its normal routine. Certainly, those of us who are old enough to have experienced the acceleration of age and time understand this. When you were ten years old, each year represents one full 10th of your life. But when you are 50, a year is a mere 2 percent of your life, and it seems to pass just as quickly. With each year and with each year's new experiences you are adding less and less new time and new experience, as a proportion of your life's total. So, in a very real way, time does in fact speed up.

So, that is the paradox of time; at once it is linear and even. Yet, at the same time it is non-linear and completely uneven. Up until now, starting from those days just before

Yanna's arrival, time had sped by. We anticipated and
prepared for her coming. We fell in love with her and
initiated the adoption process. Yes, we had to send her back,
but we also had traveled to Russia to see her twice. And,
with the passage of each and every day, we felt that we
moved closer to the final adoption. Each day it seemed, we
completed some step, accomplished some requirement,
crossed some hurdle, moved aside one more shovel full of
dirt. And time flew by. But, when Children of the World
lost its accreditation, time seemed simply to stop, and we
froze in place with it. Nothing happened because there was
nothing to do. There were no forms to complete and no calls
to make. There was no fixed date to which we could look
forward and no calendar of milestones that we could follow.
I would call Justin, periodically, just to touch base. He was
always polite, but I could tell that my calls frustrated him.
"Allen," he would say, "we still know nothing."

In my own ethnocentric view of the situation, this just
didn't make sense. We should be able make a call, to
persuade someone, to write a letter to the proper authorities,
to talk to a supervisor somewhere or find some pressure point
where we could push to move this thing forward. But there
was nothing we could do, absolutely nothing. And, so, time,
just like the gears of the adoption machinery in Russia,
seemed simply to stop cold.

Even now, it's hard for me to recall that whole period
and to do so accurately and in proper sequence and context.
It was as if we were moving through time sideways; it was

hard for us, completely bewildering for Yanna, and totally unfair to our other children. Recall they had decided to take this journey, too, but they understood less about it than we did and, so, when the excitement began to wear off, their impatience with the process and their frustration with us began to show. Their lives were moving forward normally, but their parents were somehow stuck in time. They had not seen their new sister in months, yet we were constantly talking about and planning for her return – even though we had no idea when that return would come to pass. We were reluctant to plan ahead and reluctant to make commitments, for fear that the process would suddenly restart and we could not risk being caught unprepared. We could see what was happening, and we could understand the frustrations we were causing, but there was nothing that we could do about it. People would ask what was happening, if there was anything new to report or if we were any closer to the adoption. We would simply explain the situation over and again, until we ourselves grew tired of hearing the same old story and people began to grow uncomfortable asking about it.

We also got lots of well-meaning but exceptionally insensitive and even bad advice. Perhaps my favorite bit of insensitive advice came from the international adoption community. When you're involved in a process like this, your story gets out, and you begin to meet people who are involved, or who have been involved, in the same sort of thing. As I mentioned earlier, there are many hopeful parents out there, who cannot conceive biologically and so have sought to adopt. Motivated by their desire to find a child and to complete their adoptions, these parents will seek those adoption agents and countries, who can get results the fastest and the most inexpensively. In some years, that path of least resistance led to countries like Nicarauga, Guatamela, Ukraine or even China. But then circumstances would change, and some other country would gain an informal sort of "most favored nation status" in the adoption community. During this season for us, the adoptive country of choice was Latvia. And in 2006 – 2008 at least, Latvian adoptions were happening quickly, easily and inexpensively. Meanwhile, Russian adoptions were the exact opposite of that, on every dimension, slow, difficult and expensive.

So, at least once a month, if not more often than that, some well-meaning soul would offer advice that went much like this; "you know I have a friend who just adopted a child from Latvia, and it only took them two months, start to finish. You should just go there." In response, I would try to be gracious and appreciative. But how exactly was I supposed to take this advice? Did they really think we could just turn off the love we had for Yanna? Did they really think we were just interested in adopting a child, any child? Like picking out a puppy, I suppose, perhaps they thought we were simply shopping around, looking for the best deal among the range of potential suppliers. In some ways, it was rather amusing; in other ways, it was down right infuriating; however, it was always innocent and well intentioned. So, we just explained that we were not particularly interested in adoption in general. Rather, we were intensely interested in adopting legally this one particular little girl, who we had long ago adopted fully in our hearts. No, we were committed to Russia and inextricably bound to one particular little girl, who just happened to be locked for the time at least behind an iron curtain of bureaucratic lethargy.

Some other advice we began getting was simply bad. While we were working with Children of the World, there were other adoption agencies out there, many others. Of course, these others were all unaccredited and inactive, too. Over time and the many months that it took for the process to open back up following the shut down in April, different agencies were reaccredited at different times. As a result, there would occasionally be rumors that "ABC Adoption Agency" had been reaccredited and was now able to submit adoption applications. These rumors spread like a brush fire in a drought amidst the many families circling in this holding pattern. Often times, there was never any clear origin to the rumors. We would just hear from a friend, who had heard from a friend, who had heard from someone else, that an agency in Texas or Montana or some other place other than here was reaccredited. We would even hear occasionally that some agency had just successfully completed an adoption and brought a child home.

Because they were often so unspecific, these rumors were hard to confirm or disprove. LeAnn, the director at the NHFC, the hosting agency, would try to distribute reliable information through her network. But she couldn't know everything and couldn't answer every question. Moreover, it's just in our natures to hear what we want to hear. So, in trying to explain the complexity of the situation, what we knew, what we thought and what we hoped, people sometimes heard just a portion of the message. And then they repeated that portion, exaggerating it only slightly. But then it was heard again in part and repeated again inaccurately, until a full-blown rumor, with little grounding in the facts, had emerged and taken on a life of its own.

Perhaps the most frustrating bit of misinformation that circulated involved the so-called private adoptions. These arrangements were not affected by the accrediting problems because these sorts of adoptions and adoption agents were not accredited. The private adoptions worked something like this; an adoption agent in the U.S. or elsewhere would have a contact or contacts in Russia. Those contacts, perhaps unscrupulous attorneys, business people, healthcare workers or corrupt government officials, would hear of an unwanted pregnancy. They would then reach out to the mother to see if she would be interested in putting her child up for adoption, for a price. They would then contact their counterpart in the U.S., who would work with their list of clients to place the child with an adoptive family. These sorts of adoption agents were essentially brokers, bringing together buyer and seller directly in a way that was not only illegal in Russia and many other countries, but that also provided little oversight to protect the interests of the children or the biological parents. Indeed, there are many anecdotal stories of Russian mothers who went into the delivery rooms expecting a healthy delivery, only be drugged and later told that their children had died during delivery. The suspicion was, however, that their children had simply been taken and adopted privately. Other times, mothers who were on drugs, in poverty or on the streets, would sell their services willingly, despite the potential problems their children might have had and creating a perverse incentive to use child bearing as a way to generate much needed income. The prevalence of these sorts of stories, which were sometimes based in fact, and sometimes not, contributed to the negative perception of foreign adoption in Russian society.

Of course, to the average American the distinction between a legally sanctioned and a private adoption was a matter of mere semantics. In the minds of those who would hear and retell these stories, Russian adoptions were happening. You simply had to have the right agent, with the right contacts. Once again, the story would go something like this; "I have a friend who has a friend with a cousin that recently adopted from Russia." They might even have a picture of the child to go along with the story of how they were able to complete the adoption within just two or three months of meeting the right attorney. It was tremendously frustrating, and you just had to bite your lip, acknowledge their good intentions and thank them for their help.

Sometimes it was just hard though. Occasionally we would encounter someone so sure of their sources and so convinced of their advice that they would push too far. They would say things like, why wouldn't you want to at least try this? After all, if you really love this girl, wouldn't you want to get her home as soon as possible? Of course we loved her and of course we wanted her home! But we also understood the risk. If we broke our contract with Children of the World and engaged another agent, we would lose our spot in line. We were confident that the process would, one day, open back up. When it did, we were at the top of Justin's agenda. Relinquishing that spot was a risk we were reluctant to take, but an even greater risk was being somehow linked to an illegitimate adoption agency. Suppose we contracted with one of these private parties and somehow offended the Russian adoption authorities? We could be blacklisted altogether and prevented from ever adopting a child from Russia. So, it was difficult to listen to these stories and to get this sort of advice, but to sit and do nothing.

As it turned out, I almost took some of this bad advice and left Children of the World for another agency. It was in the early Fall of 2007, I believe. The process had been shut down and our application had been frozen for two – three months. I had called Justin periodically but the story had remained largely the same. I had written to various agencies within the U.S. government asking for help. I had even reached out to the White House, to President Bush, the First Lady, and to every member of the Georgia congressional delegation, all for nothing. So, I was growing desperate when word began circulating through that network of adoptive families, that some agencies were being reaccredited. This time, though, the rumors were more specific than before and there was a name. I won't mention the actual name of the agency because I did not, ultimately, choose to work with them. But they were a legitimate agency, with a real contact name, a phone number, and a history of doing licensed adoptions in Russia.

I remember calling them and speaking with the agency manager for over an hour. I was on a business trip to Nashville TN, and called from the car as I drove on I-24. I explained our situation, and she listened. She had heard of NHFC, the hosting agency that brought Yanna to us. She had worked before with families from NHFC and had had some success. Her agency, too, had lost its accreditation, as part of this same large-scale review. In fact, her agency was still unaccredited, just like ours; however, she was convinced that they would receive the good news of their reaccreditation soon. Moreover, she explained that they did not have a queue in which we would have to wait if we were to come over and sign with her agency. Instead, they simply submitted dossiers to the Russian government as soon as those dossiers were ready. And, given how much work we had already done, our dossier would likely be submitted first, or nearly so.

I can still recall this conversation and my feelings afterward. The temptation and pressure, along with the risks, were extraordinary. Would this other agency truly be reaccredited soon, and would it be reaccredited before

Children of the World? If so, would our dossier be among the first submitted? What about the quality of the service? Would we be advised properly on the assembly of our dossier, and would the agency's people in Russia deliver the good services and results promised? A good decision could potentially gain us quite a lot. A bad decision could cost us everything. So, we thought about it, prayed about it and thought about it some more. We sought the wise counsel of our trusted friends, but their opinions differed and none was conclusive. It was finally Mike the Russian missionary who provided the key bit of information.

While discussing the situation with him, and asking his opinion, he offered a phrase that still sticks in my head. Justin, he said, was able "to get results where others weren't." Now, Mike did not know Justin. In fact, they would not meet until the Summer of 2008, when I would introduce them over coffee, in the lobby of the Hotel Moscow, in St. Petersburg. Nevertheless, Mike was very familiar with adoptions of Russian children in St. Petersburg, and, so, he was also familiar with the intricacies of the process and with some of the agencies that effectively navigated it. And, so, he offered this assessment; he was not familiar with this other agency, and he knew nothing about the pace or sequencing of the reaccreditations. But he had heard of Children of the World and of Justin. He had heard that Justin could be difficult interpersonally and that he submitted only a very limited number of dossiers at any one time. Mostly, though, Mike had heard that Justin got results.

Indeed, even where others had had difficulty, Justin got results. And what we wanted were results. So, after thorough and heart-wrenching consideration, we chose to pass on this other option and stay with Children of the World.

I remember calling Justin to tell him that I had investigated other options but had chosen to remain with him. He was not surprised nor was he either angry or happy about any of this. As I explained earlier, Justin is his own magnetic north, and he doesn't change much in response to the circumstances around him. He simply said that he hoped I had made the right choice and that he would be in touch when he finally received good news from Moscow. I can still remember asking "And, when do you think that will be?" His response was classically Justin, "Who knows…" he said.

Milestones and Breadcrumbs

This period of time and testing would last at least eight months. I say at least because it's not quite clear when it officially ended. Of course, we finalized our adoption of Yanna in March of 2008, and we finally brought her home to stay in April of the same year. That was fully a year after my first visit and after the process had shut down. But long before the adoption was final, we began to get good news and to see some positive changes. The first of those positive events was in November, of 2007, when we found out that we would be able to host Yanna again for a Christmas visit. Of course, this second visit would be very different from the first. This time, Yanna would be home with her family for Christmas. That was a good time.

But long before we learned about that second hosting, we had to endure a period of seven to nine months, from late March through to November of 2007. During this period, we made no progress on the adoption at all. There was no new information from Justin, no new paperwork completed, no additional steps taken whatsoever. It was as if an order of radio silence had been issued, during which we simply stood still and waited. It was absolutely terrible. But I mark it now with the memories of actions we took on our own. We were convinced that Yanna was our daughter and so we acted accordingly. We approached this time just as we would have, had any of our other children been away in another country. We called her often. I even became somewhat proficient with my rudimentary Russian. I could call the orphanage and introduce myself. I could then ask to speak with Yanna and thank the receptionist for his or her assistance. We would then chat briefly, before saying her bedtime prayers. That just became our tradition and we called most every evening before she went to bed. We sent her a letter or some small gift, typically once or twice per month. Here again, we had learned the address of the orphanage and learned how to package things so that they would arrive reliably and safely. And, we would ask Sasha to stop by the orphanage periodically to check on Yanna and to take her out for the day. On some occasions Sasha was able to get Yanna for an entire weekend. When the timing worked, we would call Yanna while she was with Sasha, that way, Sasha could translate. Mike and Olga would sometimes do the same thing, take Yanna out of the orphanage and keep her at their home for a weekend. While Yanna was there, Mike would often Skype us so that we could see our little girl while we talked to her.

As useful as these things were, though, they simply weren't enough. How many of us could be content speaking to our children only a few times a week or sending them letters only a couple of times a month? Especially with Yanna being so young and having had her trust shattered by her biological parents and by a bureaucratic system of foster homes and orphanages, we simply could not allow her to think that she had been abandoned by us as well. We had to do more than be merely good pen pals. Like the good parents we were to our other children, we had to be present in and a regular part of her life. And so we committed to travel to Russia as often as necessary to make that a reality.

So, during this period between Yanna's first visit and her second, Cricket and I together traveled to Russia six different times. For us, these trips were the milestones by which we measured our progress. The adoption process was frozen but the parenting process was not. With each visit, our relationship to Yanna strengthened, as did our understanding of her needs and personality. For Yanna, these trips, along with the calls, letters and gifts, were like breadcrumbs, showing her the way home. With each visit, Yanna grew to trust us and grew to see us as her father and mother. And it was on my way home from one of those trips that I wrote the next installment on my newsletter.

September 21, 2007

I wanted to give you an update on Yanna and the adoption process. I chose now to write because, at this moment, I am flying home from St. Petersburg, Russia. I was there for 7 full days, visiting friends, cultivating some business opportunities, and, of course, visiting our little girl.

At present, the adoption process is still closed, at least for us and our agency. As you recall, Russia did not reaccredit any international adoption agencies when their licenses expired last year. Thus, since April when our agency's license expired, we have been in a holding pattern. We have all the necessary U.S. approvals and paperwork, but are unable to submit our adoption application to the Russian government. It has been a frustrating time and a humbling one. I have always prided myself on my ability to make things happen, to out wit or out maneuver any constraint. Yet, despite my strong motivation, nothing I have done has changed the situation. So, I have come to accept that this process is truly in God's hands and that I am totally dependent on Him.

We visit when we can. Cricket visited Yanna in St. Petersburg in January and at a summer camp by the Black Sea in June. I visited in April and now again in September, both times in St. Petersburg. These visits have been great. For a few days Yanna has her parents and we have our daughter. Of course, those days pass, the visit ends and we have to leave. Indeed, I did that just last night; I took Yanna back to the orphanage, hugged her,

*reassured her, told her we loved her, and then I
said goodbye.*

*Still, as hard as it was, it was worth it for the time
we had together. We went bowling and ice
skating; we watched movies on my computer and
took a row boat out on a lake. For a few days and
hours she was a normal little girl, enjoying life
with her daddy at her side, protecting her and
providing for her. For now, that is all we have.
And while we thank God for it, we still pray for
more. The desire of our hearts is that Yanna will
come home soon and for good, to a family that
loves her and to a home that is prepared for her.
And, just as we have learned that this process is
fully in God's hands, so too do we look only to
Him for deliverance. And we ask that you please
join us in praying for Yanna and our family.*

*Thank you for your prayers and support
throughout. There are signs that the process may
be soon restarting. We hope and pray that is the
case and we hope to have some good news for you
very soon. We covet your prayers.*

Blessings,

Allen

Because most of these trips followed a pattern similar
to what I described before, I won't relay the details of each
one specifically. In fact, as I mentioned earlier, so much
about this time is now blurred it's difficult to recall it all
anyway. What I do recall is that my trips usually had some
work related purpose; I would lecture at St. Petersburg
Christian University, meet with the faculty in the business

school at St. Petersburg State University, give a speech at the meeting of a trade association or business group. It was really a time of significant intellectual, as well as spiritual, growth for me. I became very comfortable in Russia and began to appreciate its history and people. I grew to appreciate a great deal about the business world outside of the U.S. and Western Europe. In any language, the basics of business are fundamentally the same. But the reality of the context creates some unique pressures and forces some unique adaptations. So, these visits were important to our parenting of Yanna, but they were also important to my own understanding and growth.

Cricket's visits were typically more emotionally rich, as they were focused entirely on parenting. On one trip she called me, via Skype, from Mike and Olga's apartment. My expectation was that she would put Yanna on the line, so that the three of us could see and talk to one another. That wasn't to be though. As Cricket explained, Yanna had crawled under the bed and was still there, crying. She had wanted something and Cricket, like a good mother, had decided the time wasn't right and so told Yanna "no." Dealing with this sort of parental authority was a new experience, and it frustrated Yanna. She expressed her frustration with crying and lying under the bed. So, the opportunity to speak on the computer was missed. This is just normal parenting, of course. But, when your time with your child is so limited and so precious, you become keenly aware of the value of each moment. I often struggled as a result, not wanting to waste a second of my time in Russia by fighting over something trivial, and, so, I often gave in when Yanna would get frustrated or angry. Cricket, in her wisdom, took a longer view and looked ahead to the many years that would follow. We were now Yanna's parents; we would have to make decisions about her welfare, and she would have to learn to respect and trust us in those decisions.

But we had to earn that trust and respect. We had to be steadfast in showing our love, even when the circumstances were so utterly discouraging. We had to demonstrate to her that there was zero chance that we would change our minds or that we would lose interest, as some prospective parents had done. We had to be confident and to reassure Yanna that we would be there for her, laws and bureaucracies aside. We were Yanna's parents, and we would adopt her as our daughter. Even if the system failed us, we had to be prepared to move to Russia, if that is what it took. We had to provide for her and to fill in the gaps where the orphanage or the government failed to provide for all her needs. Mostly though, we had to be present in her life, as often and as consistently as we could. Sometimes that was easy and fun but other times it was not. One particular trip that was not fun was Cricket's trip to Taganrog.

Life in an orphanage can be monotonous and trying for the children and for their caregivers. So, the system provided relief in the form of a summer vacation. Most every summer, at most every orphanage across Russia, the kids and a subset of the adult caregivers would pack up their things, board a train or a bus and head out to summer camp, at some remote location. These camps typically lasted about two months. Sometimes the camps were nice and a fun time for the kids; other times they were not very nice and were ordeals that simply had to be endured. But even when they were difficult, they served an important purpose. They provided a change of pace for the kids and an opportunity for the children to socialize with children from other orphanages across Russia. They provided a change of venue for the caregivers. While not exactly vacations for these adults, they were an opportunity to get out of the city, to change the pace of their routine and to see another part of the country at government expense. They also offered an opportunity to make repairs or improvements to the orphanage without disrupting the children. It was during these summer camps that the building would be repainted, that the electrical or heating systems would be fixed or that the roof would be replaced. So, these camps and summer vacations were important to the system and a normal part of the life in the orphanages.

For us, though, this particular summer vacation looked like a dark and ominous cloud looming on the horizon, and it struck me with a thick sense of dread. You see, during these two months, it was altogether likely that we would have no contact with Yanna whatsoever. I remember sending a message to the orphanage director, through Sasha, asking if we could pay to send Yanna to a private camp, somewhere near a major city. While there we could visit her, or at least call her as we were now doing regularly. The director said, "no;" Yanna needed to be with her friends and her counselors. That made good sense, but it didn't solve the problem. So, we asked if Cricket could go to the camp and visit Yanna there. This time, the answer was, "yes," which meant that Cricket would be going to a place called Taganrog.

Taganrog is near a town called Rostov-on-Don, close to Sochi, where the winter Olympics were held. Sochi is on the Black Sea, but Taganrog is on the Sea of Azov, a body of water just off the Black Sea. It is a shallow and relatively warm body of water that is bordered by Russia and Ukraine. The Sea of Azov serves ports in both countries, is fed mainly by the Don and Kuban rivers, and drains into the Black Sea through the narrow Straight of Kerch. Because of its location and geological characteristics, the Sea of Azov is a somewhat dirty and uninviting body of water, with heavy industrial traffic and lots of dead fish. The city of Taganrog has about a quarter of a million residents and is the native home of the great Russian author Anton Chekov. It was a city of some maritime and industrial significance until the 1940s and 50s, when changes in Russian society began to pass it by. It is now a sleepy little city, or large town, off the beaten path but on the water in far southwestern Russia. The camp was an old communist youth camp and was right on the water, a few miles to the west of the city.

I tell you all of this to illustrate the logistical and cultural challenge this visit presented. How does one even get to Taganrog, and, once there, how does one get around? We had decided that Cricket would be the one to go. After all, we still had three other children who needed us at home. We wanted to conserve our resources, and, by making our trips independently, we were able to make more trips. We also knew that we would have to make at least two trips to Russia together once the process reopened and the actual adoption got fully underway. So, we decided that only Cricket would make this trip, and she would make it without me. We did have our ace in the hole, though; we had Sasha.

The plan unfolded something like this. Sasha made the arrangements with the orphanage director. Cricket and Sasha would visit the camp and live as guests with the children for about two weeks. I made the flight arrangements; Cricket would fly from Atlanta to Moscow, and Sasha would fly to Moscow from St. Petersburg. They would meet there, where they would together board a flight to Rostov. Sasha would arrange ground transportation for the one-hour ride to Taganrog, where I had booked them a night in what appeared to be a somewhat clean, modern hotel. After that first night, they were pretty much on their own. They had to find a way to the camp; they had to find the director and get themselves situated, and they had to find a way to feed and care for themselves while they were there. As I said, it was a challenge. And it became all the more so after about a week when Sasha came down with the flu.

I was able to call and talk to Cricket via Sasha's cell phone. But calling was expensive, and the service was generally poor. Based on what I could discern, though, Cricket and Sasha were housed in a room in the dormitory where the children lived. That was good, and it afforded Yanna the opportunity to spend a lot of time with her mom. Beyond that, though, there was little about this trip that will be remembered fondly. Sasha came down with a raging case of the flu and was out of commission for several days with high fever and body aches. It was very hot, and the building was not air-conditioned. The windows were large but they opened only at the very top and they were positioned in such a way that they provided little cross-ventilation. Food was a problem, as the camp was set up to serve about 1,000 orphans and their caregivers; however, it was not set up for tourists. So Cricket and Sasha were not given access to the cafeteria. While they would occasionally have things brought to them by the children or by the orphanage workers, they mostly had to go into town to buy food that could be kept and prepared in their room. They did enjoy a lot of time with Yanna and her friends. They would take them swimming in the Sea of Azov, take them into Taganrog for the day, or play games with them at night in the room. But only a small fraction of the children at the camp were from Yanna's orphanage. The rest tended to view these visitors with some suspicion. Indeed, someone actually broke into their room one day and took money from Cricket's suitcase. On top of all that, several of the children, including Yanna and her roommates, got lice in the camp and had to be deloused. So, it was a hard visit.

Of course, the parting was even harder. When it came time for Cricket to leave, Yanna began to grow resentful and angry. In fact, during the final day or two at the camp, Yanna would often avoid her mom, almost as if she didn't want to have to say good-bye. And the logistics of the return trip did not help to ease the pain of parting. Cricket was detained by an officer at the Rostov airport; the purpose of this delay was little more than a shakedown. The officer insisted that Cricket's visa was out of order and that she would have to pay a fine. Of course, her visa was in perfect order and this agent wanted nothing more than a bribe. As it turned out, Cricket had little left with which to bribe the corrupt officer anyway because of the theft that had occurred at the camp. Sasha came to the rescue, turning the tables on this officer by asking if she could simply return home and leave Cricket there. The officer, not wanting to be stuck with an American, who had no money and no ability to speak Russian quickly relented and let the two of them pass. The trip home was long, from Rostov to Moscow and then back to St. Petersburg for Sasha and Atlanta for Cricket. Both were tired and hungry, and both looked forward to their own beds and to a nice shower. What is more, they left without many hugs or kisses from Yanna.

On one of their trips into the town of Taganrog, Cricket purchased an inexpensive cell phone for Yanna. She sent me the number, and I called it several times before she left the camp. But it never worked very well. As I mentioned, the coverage out at the camp was poor, and this phone was not of the highest quality. Still, it would provide us with a lifeline to Yanna. At least we would be able talk to her, or so we thought. I remember calling it on the day Cricket left the camp. Yanna answered; either she was in a bad mood or the connection was especially poor, perhaps both. But we had a tough time communicating. I asked to speak to her mother and all I could understand in return was Yanna saying, "mom gone." That was July 13 of 2007, and that was the last we heard from our little girl for the rest of the summer.

Once the children returned to the orphanage in late August we were able to reach Yanna again. But we could tell that she was much more distant and cold. We later found out that she was hurt that we had quit calling her. What she did not know, what she couldn't have known at the time, was that her phone had quit working altogether. We tried; we tried the phone number often, in the hopes that it had spontaneously started working again. We tried to find the camp and to call it directly; we tried every way imaginable to call her but nothing ever worked, and we eventually gave up. We simply couldn't get through. We had been told that the kids were due to return to St. Petersburg in late August. So, late in August, we tried calling the number again. Quite randomly, we got an answer one day; however, the person on the other end was an adult and a complete stranger. In Russian, I asked for Yanna; they said I had the wrong number. So, I called back and asked again for Yanna. Again, and this time quite explicitly, the person who answered the phone told me this was not Yanna's number and then hung up. It was terribly discouraging. As Yanna would later tell us, some time after the phone quit working, it was stolen or lost. So, the number was likely reassigned. The end result of this all was that Yanna had felt abandoned and she was somewhat hurt and resentful.

Unfortunately, there was no simple way to explain all of this to her. Even if my Russian had been good enough, which it was not, Yanna was in no mood to listen. The only solution was to get her home and into the routine of a normal childhood; however, we couldn't move forward with the adoption until our agency was licensed and, at this point, no agency was yet relicensed. So, we had no choice but to continue to wait, to pray, and to send Cricket on another trip to Russia.

The Wall Comes Down

It was late in October of 2007 when Cricket made her final solo visit to St. Petersburg. She stayed a week at the home of Mike and Olga and was able to get Yanna out of the orphanage for most of the time. They would take walks, do some shopping, make meals together, all the things a little girl might expect to do with her mother. Often, in the late evenings, they would get on Mike's computer and call me via Skype. I mention this only because one particular call was the episode I had mentioned earlier. Cricket had called me and we had spent a few minutes talking about this and that. She finally asked me, "would you like to talk to Yanna?" I replied yes, of course. "Well, you can't. You see, she's having a temper tantrum and is under the bed in her room, and she won't come out." Kids will be kids, I suppose, and this instance was nothing out of the ordinary for a ten year old. So, while this was a rather unremarkable occurrence, for me it was an especially regrettable one because it was an opportunity lost.

More importantly, it was another instance that underscored for me the urgency of our situation. We needed to get Yanna home. She needed to learn to appreciate and understand parental love and authority. Lord willing, we would always provide her with everything she needed, but she needed to learn to appreciate and trust that. She would have ample opportunity to get the things she wanted to learn how to decide for herself which things were right. She would learn that a "no" from her mother sometimes actually meant "wait." She would develop an understanding that her parents, though imperfect, had her best interests at heart and made decisions for her, based on their desire to see her grow into the adult she was created to be. These are lessons that most of us spend our childhood learning. Yanna, though, was growing up without the opportunity to learn any of this. And as she got older, more and more of that opportunity slipped away.

There are many stories of adoptions involving older children that simply turned out badly. In some of these cases, the children rebelled against the parents' authority and rules. In some cases they couldn't adjust to living in a family, and they couldn't learn to trust the security of their new setting. Sometimes, the parents had trouble relating to their new child and struggled to accept this child who came to their family with a fully developed personality.

Sometimes, the children had physical or psychological disorders associated with the dysfunctions of their biological families or with the limitations and harshness of orphanage life. These stories were all too commonly heard in and among our circle of friends and acquaintances in this world of adoptive families. We were convinced that Yanna was our daughter, that she would fit perfectly in our family and that we could parent her well. But we had to get her home, or we had to take our home to her.

If that sounds strange, it shouldn't. For the sake of our lost child, we contemplated a move to Russia. I suspect that most parents would consider the same thing. Suppose the process never opened up, and our agency was never reaccredited? Suppose the Russian government decided to ban all foreign adoptions? This isn't so farfetched, given that the government did just that in 2013. Just suppose, some circumstance occurred whereby Yanna was not allowed to leave Russia until she reached the age of 18, or older. Allowing her to remain there, without parents, would mean abandoning all of that opportunity to grow up secure in the knowledge of her parents' love and safe within the boundaries of their guidance. We simply were not willing to do that. So, had the worst case ever become the only case, we were prepared to move our family to Russia. Of course, that was not our preference, but we were prepared for it, should it become necessary. Thankfully, it never became necessary. In fact, it seemed that, at the moment of our greatest desperation, cracks began to develop in the wall that had separated us from daughter.

The first of those cracks came in the form of a reaccreditation. Now, the agency that was reaccredited was not ours. It worked in the region surrounding Moscow, not St. Petersburg, and it did not work in the area of older children adoptions. So, hearing about it was of no specific benefit to us. Still, it was a crack in the wall, and it gave us hope. The second crack came in the form of a phone call from LeAnn. She asked, "are you planning to host Yanna for Christmas again this year?" Host again? We were not even sure that would be possible. We had talked with Mike about it. But he was uncertain, uncertain the government would allow the hosting program to take place for another year and uncertain, even if it was allowed, that Yanna would be selected and assigned to us. LeAnn, on the other hand, was optimistic. We simply needed to complete the process again, just as we had the year before. And, just as we had the year before, we needed to choose Yanna as the child we would like to host.

Of course, if we were talking about hosting here in the States, then you know the children in Russia were talking about it, too. In fact, it was about this time, in the middle of the fall 2007, that Yanna began asking us, in her broken English "Yanna America Christmas?" Well, even had we known that she was coming, which we did not, we could not yet tell her. Indeed, it was a condition of the hosting process and a real priority of Mike's organization that the children not know that they were assigned for hosting until they were all told together. So, until we got the approval, all we could do was answer her questions with "ya ney poneymyou" or "I don't know." Oh, that was so sad and it was made even more so by the fact that we could tell that it made Yanna sad, too.

It's amusing to look back now, though. One reason is because Yanna has now told us that she already knew she had been assigned to be hosted for Christmas. How she knew I'm not quite sure, but it shouldn't be surprising that children talk about things like this. So, I'm sure rumors ran rampant through the orphanage at this time of year. And, certainly, some of those rumors actually proved true on occasion. So, Yanna and many of the other children knew that they would be hosted, they simply didn't know by whom. So, every time Yanna would ask us her question, she wanted confirmation that we were the family to which she was being assigned. We simply did what we had been told to do and stonewalled and told her that we didn't know. So, either we seemed to her to be the dumbest parents in the world, or she suspected that she had been assigned to another family. Sometimes, in an imperfect world, full of imperfect individuals, things can just be confused and difficult and I suppose this was just one of those things.

Eventually, though, we were allowed to tell her and eventually she did come back for the same sort of five-week visit as the one we had enjoyed in 2006. While the schedule was largely the same, the rest of the visit was very different. It's not that we were less excited. Quite the contrary, we were thrilled. We picked her up at the airport and recognized her immediately. She came running to us and couldn't wait to leave the airport and head home. We were also much better known to the hosting agency and so much more trusted with Yanna's well being. We didn't have to check in as often and didn't have to attend all of those organized group events. Also, because Yanna now spoke some English and I now spoke some Russian, we had a much easier time communicating. What is more, because Yanna now knew we were planning to adopt her, there was no secret to keep, no having to use code words like "project platypus" and no reason not to begin introducing her to her new extended family. Before she arrived, I sent the note below to those who were receiving my newsletter.

December 6, 2007

Lord willing, Yanna will arrive in 6 days and we are more excited than words can describe. You may recall that we have not been able to confirm to her that she was coming, even though she has asked us about it. It has been hard on us but it has been especially hard on her. She was actually wondering whether she was being hosted by a different family. Well, that changed yesterday! We received word that she had been officially informed and that it was now okay for us to discuss it with her. So, we called and what a phone call that was! She is so happy to be coming and we, of course, are so thankful to have her home, even for a short time.

She will depart St. Petersburg next Wednesday morning with 10 other children and 2 chaperones from Russia. They will arrive in Atlanta late Wednesday afternoon and we have told Yanna to expect to see us the moment she comes up the escalator. There will also be 50 children and 4 chaperones coming from Latvia. Please pray for all these kids, the families, and the program. This is such a great opportunity and I am excited for everyone involved.

I ask you though especially for prayer for Yanna and for the adoption process. We heard today that our agency was not among those reaccredited in late November. This was a bitter disappointment as we had been told to expect good news. Indeed, it seems that there have still been no new adoptions initiated for older children since last April. The emotional burden on the families and the children is terrible; honestly it's difficult to talk about even in a forum like this. So, I simply ask that you pray, for the program and the children yes, but specifically for Yanna and for us. We need a special touch from God; in short, we need a miracle.

But our hope is in the One who has the power to transform, to save, and to bring our daughter home. Through scripture, God tells us "Do not be afraid for I am with you; I will bring your children from the east and gather you from the west" (Is. 43: 5). Our hope is in Him and we look forward to His promised deliverance. Thank you for your perseverance.

Blessings,

Allen

For this visit, we planned an extended trip. The day after Christmas we would leave and head first to coastal Georgia, where Yanna would visit two of her three sets of grandparents. After a visit there, we would head to Florida, where we would spend four days at the Disney World resorts. We were very excited about the trip, and, so, were a bit disappointed to learn that Yanna had never heard of Disney World and was not particularly excited to learn that she would soon be going. No bother, though, she would learn soon enough. One other side benefit of this trip was that we would have the opportunity to take lots of pictures of Yanna with her new, loving family. We had been advised by our adoption agent that the Russian court would require pictures of us, pictures of our home and pictures of us interacting together, happily. So it seemed natural that we'd want to take lots of pictures while Yanna was with us on a family trip.

We also continued our Christmas movie night tradition. Recall that in the previous year, 2006, we had gone to see Cirque du Soleil. This year, however, we decided to go see the Nutcracker by the Atlanta Ballet. Our thinking was that the Nutcracker is not only a traditional Christmas favorite but was also written by a famous Russian composer. So, we made plans to go and to take with us two of the adult Russian chaperones who came with the children on the hosting program. In the previous year, the director of Yanna's orphanage had been among the chaperones. The families who host the children often volunteer to take turns chaperoning the chaperones during their visit. These adults really appreciated the change of venue, and it was good for them to see the children with their host families. So, in the previous year, we had invited the director to our house for a couple of days. In 2007, though, no adult from Yanna's orphanage was on the trip. Still, other adults employed at other orphanages around St. Petersburg were there. So, we offered to have two women join us for a night on the town in Atlanta. We picked them up at a church northwest of town, took them shopping and to dinner, took them to the ballet and then dropped them off at the home of some other host parents.

While it was just one night and now many years in the past, four things about the evening still stand out in my memory. The first thing was that we nearly died at the hands of one of the chaperones. The woman, named Tatiana, asked me if she could drive our car. I suppose she just wanted the experience of driving in America. By this point, I had been to Russia many times and knew that many Russians owned and drove cars. Tatiana assured me she was a very good driver and even showed me her Russian driver's license. So, I agreed to let her drive from a suburb northwest of Atlanta into downtown. That was a mistake I regret to this day. To say the experience was harrowing would be to understate the reality. Oh, my goodness. It was a white-knuckled affair, with screams and screeches aplenty, before I finally convinced Tatiana to pull over and relinquish the wheel.

The second thing was the shopping. Both women had told us that they wanted to do some shopping for family and friends back in St. Petersburg. So, we took them first to Target, but they quickly conveyed to us that their tastes were decidedly more upscale. So, we left Target and went to Lenox Square, a trendy shopping mall in the toney Buckhead region of Atlanta. This was more their taste and both spent significant sums of money, several thousand dollars each, on designer apparel. I was later told that they would take these items back to Russia and sell them for a tidy profit. While I have nothing against commerce and entrepreneurship, I have to admit being a bit surprised by this. We thought we were being charitable and helping these women, who had agreed to help bring the host children to America. As it turns out, this was all business for them. Oh, well, we got the result we wanted and these women were instrumental in bringing that about. So I shouldn't begrudge them making a few dollars along the way. I'm just glad our minivan could hold all the clothes they purchased.

The third thing I remember was the show itself. While clearly up to my standards, if not even over my head, it was a bit simplistic in the eyes of our Russian guests. I'm not sure what I was thinking in putting this evening together. Russia is home to many of the world's greatest dancers. Ballet is taught in Russian schools from an early age and Russian culture is steeped with stories of greats like Mikhail Barishnykov and Galina Ulanova. So, a performance that would impress me might leave a sophisticated Russian underwhelmed. And, apparently these two Russian women were quite sophisticated and underwhelmed. While I didn't discuss it with them directly and while they were generally polite, I was able to overhear and understand some of their comments. They thought the dancers were mediocre; they thought the sets were overly simple and, most of all, they were disappointed that there was no live music. Now, I have to give it to them on this last point. The Atlanta Ballet dancing the Nutcracker suite at the historic and beautiful Fox Theatre, to canned music. It was a little embarrassing. Oh, well, we tried, and they seemed to appreciate that. Moreover, it was a night on the town, with a new and different set of people, enjoying a new and different set of experiences. All in all, it was mission accomplished for them and for us.

The fourth and final thing I remember from that night occurred as we were returning Tatiana, the woman who had driven our car, home to the next host family who would be keeping her. It was at least 10:00 p.m., and we were all tired from our long, and briefly harrowing, day. We had a car full of baggage from the shopping excursion at Lenox Square, and we were crowded anyway, with the six of us and our two guests, all in our seven passenger minivan. So, we were ready to be home and ready for the night to end. Yet, somewhere someone was still working. And that someone decided to call me.

When my cell phone rang, it came as something of a surprise. No one at work would be calling at this hour, and my wife and children were all with me in the car. Still, I struggled to take the phone out of my pocket and looked at the number; it was Justin. So I answered quickly. "Allen," he said with his thick accent. "I have just received word from my agent in Moscow that our agency has been reaccredited. I will have the official paperwork tomorrow but, as soon as we have it, Phyllis will call you to begin putting together your dossier for submission to Russia." As best I recall, I nearly cried as months of stress and waiting began to lift. I thanked Justin and hung up the phone. Then, I told everyone in the car what had just happened. We cheered with the energy typically reserved for a football game. We dropped off Tatiana and soon thereafter dropped off the other chaperone, Ludmilla, as well. We then drove home, excited about the future.

The rest of Yanna's visit, Christmas 2007, was as pleasant and uneventful as we could have hoped for. Indeed, it actually felt like our family was complete and together. We did spend several days traveling to visit Yanna's new grandparents. We introduced her to everyone as our daughter and explained that we would be adopting her in the spring of the year. We took her in a boat to a deserted beach on one of Georgia's uninhabited barrier islands. We took her to the pier on St. Simons Island and we took lots of pictures.

We rented an enormous SUV for our drive to coastal Georgia and then onto Florida. The SUV had an integrated TV / DVD player, which allowed the kids to watch movies as we drove. Cricket and I loved every minute of watching them interact and have fun together. We called Cricket's brother, who lives near Tampa, Florida, to drive up and visit us in Orlando. It was a great chance for Yanna to meet another of her new and aunts and uncles, along with several more of her new cousins. The trip to Disney world was also a blessing and a blast. All four of the kids had a ball riding the rides and seeing the shows, as we worked the parks from opening to close. The fireworks were amazing on New Year's Eve, and each night we returned to hotel completely satisfied and completely exhausted. By the time we left Orlando and began the trip back, we were ready to be home and ready to start the next, and hopefully the final, step in our long journey.

Of course, we still had to send Yanna back to Russia, but this time it was different. First of all, we knew it wouldn't be long before she returned. The process was now open, and we were at the front of the line. Second, we knew that this would be the last time we would have to send her back. And, even more importantly, we knew that she knew this. In fact, after taking Yanna to the airport for the second time, we hugged her and kissed her good bye. We then overheard, as she told one of her Russian friends, "I'm coming back soon."

January 7, 2008

I'm sorry to have been out of touch for so long but we have been very busy. What a blessing this season has been! Thank you for your prayers for Yanna and for our family. She has had a terrific time with us and we have had a blessed time with

173

her. Honestly, I could not have asked for more. We celebrated Christmas together. We got up early, had breakfast again at Waffle House, and exchanged gifts. Yanna was delighted and delightful throughout. She was able to spend time with all of her grandparents and to see where Cricket and I grew up. We were also able to take her on a boat ride from the north end of St. Simons to the edge of the Atlantic Ocean, where we walked on a deserted beach, picking shells and chasing sea gulls.

After that, we took a family vacation to Disney World. For 4 full days Yanna and the rest of the family enjoyed the Magic Kingdom, EPCOT, and the other parks. While there, we discovered that Yanna loves roller coasters! Her favorite ride was the Tower of Terror – all four kids rode that one together, while Cricket and I watched from a safe distance. She loved the New Year's Eve fireworks, which were amazing by the way. She was thrilled by the pool and the jacuzzi in our hotel; she even enjoyed traveling in the car, watching movies and stopping to eat fast food! In every way, she was just like any of our other children, but with an accent! Indeed, she bonded well with her brothers and sister and she knows very well that we are her family.

So, it will be hard to say goodbye when she leaves for Russia on Wednesday. But we will not grieve as those who have no hope. Indeed, just before Christmas we received word that our agency had been reaccredited! That was the greatest gift we could have asked for, the one thing that we really wanted. With that, we are now preparing to submit our adoption dossier to the Russian government. Our expectation is that our paperwork will go in sometime in mid to late

January. We will then travel to Russia for our first official visit sometime in early February. If all goes well, we could have Yanna home by Easter! So Wednesday will be a sad day but it will not be like last year. Rather, Yanna will leave knowing she has a home here, knowing she has a family that loves her and knowing that we intend to come for her soon.

I close this update then asking only that you continue to pray. We have been so blessed by this visit, so thankful to have had this opportunity, and we are so excited that the process is moving again. We give God all praise and glory for the great things he has done and we thank you all for your faithfulness. Please pray for Yanna as she travels on Wednesday and please continue to agree with us that God will bring her home and restore our family soon.

Blessings,

Allen

The Beginning of the End: Act One

Adopting from Russia is typically a five-step process. First, you have to be approved by the U.S. government to adopt a child and to adopt a child from a foreign country. We had crossed that bridge early in 2007, and the approval was good for a period of several years. So, we were in good shape. Second, you needed to assemble a dossier, which is a daunting collection of documents required by the government of the foreign country. Of course, we had nearly completed our dossier back in the Spring of 2007. So we simply needed to update some of the various forms and letters. Every country requires different documentation in their adoption dossiers, but all are designed for essentially the same purpose, to assure the government that the adopting family is able, willing and committed to care for the adopted child. That's a pretty tall order, and it requires a pretty tall stack of documents. I mean we had to prove everything, that we were married, that we were not criminals, that neither we nor our other children had any serious health problems, that I was employed and had the financial wherewithal to care for another child. On top of all this, not only did we have to provide the documents proving these things, we also had to provide proof that our documents were legitimate. Now, how were we supposed to do that? Well, every one of these dozens of documents had to be both notarized and apostilled.

I remember asking, when I first heard the term, just what is an apostille? Well, in actuality it is little more than a stamp, but that stamp signifies that the document has been reviewed and judged to be authentic by the U.S. State Department. Apparently, as part of the Hague Convention of 1961, more than 100 countries agreed to be part of the apostille convention. Hence, all of these countries agreed to accept the legitimacy of documents that have been apostilled. Every state in the union has at least one office for authenticating documents and providing apostilles. Georgia actually has two. The office you use depends upon why you are using it. For the purposes of international adoption, we had to go to an office in Atlanta, where we would drop off our documents, pay a small fee of about $3 per document, and then find a way to kill a few hours before we could come back and pick up our documents, which were all now affixed with a shiny gold seal and bound by this neat little brass rivet. By the time everything was assembled and apostilled, the dossier was a stack about two inches thick. The Russian government required the originals. So, I made lots of copies before sending the originals to Justin via FedEx.

Submitting the dossiers was not quite as simple as it sounds. Rather than send the completed dossiers to Russia via some company like FedEx, UPS, or DHL, Justin preferred to have them hand delivered. But traveling to Russia was expensive and took considerable forethought and planning. So, his plan was to use his clients, many of whom were traveling to Russia anyway, as private couriers. Our documents were carried by a family who had submitted their dossier back in the Fall of 2006, before the suspension of accreditation. This family had first hosted in 2005 and was, essentially, a year ahead of us. And, because they had gotten their dossier in before the closure, they were now nearly through the process and were traveling to St. Petersburg for the court hearing that would finalize their adoption. Before that hearing though, they would hand deliver a package containing our dossier to Nina, who was Justin's agent in St. Petersburg. Nina would actually file our dossier in the appropriate office in St. Petersburg.

Once the dossier was completed and filed, you were ready to move to step three. In that step, you were summoned to Russia for your "first" visit. This visit took about a week and involved a number of steps. You would meet with an office of the Russian agency that oversaw orphans and adoptions. Here you would confirm your interest in the child, sign some forms and pay some fees. You would also have a complete and thorough physical exam at a Russian hospital. You would be interviewed by a Russian social worker, as well as by a healthcare professional. And you would be part of a process where a social worker interviewed the child. There were also a variety of other things you do during this step, too, such as get the pictures that would be needed for your child's passport and visa, when you got to step four.

Step four was the actual court hearing. In most instances, this was accomplished in just one day, perhaps just a couple of hours. The problem was that the hearing was not even scheduled until everything had been completed and processed from step three. So, it was typical to travel to Russia for step three, to spend a week or so there, doing all the things I described above, only to then go back home and wait again to be summoned to the court. And it goes without saying that during all of this, your life was completely on hold.

I will explain more about the fifth and final step later. For now, let's return to that first official trip to Russia, what I am calling the beginning of the end. I can still remember the day I got the call. It was late January in 2008 and I was in NYC, consulting with a client whose office was just off Herald Square in midtown Manhattan. It was cold and rainy, and I had spent the past several days working through some difficult issues with this client traveling between their offices in Manhattan and Trenton, New Jersey. We were on a break and, as amusing as is may now seem, I had gone to the restroom when the call from Justin came. "Allen" he said, "we have a date for your meeting with the committee." This was Justin's way of saying it was time for us to make that first official trip. We were about to take step three. About a week later, I wrote the following letter.

February 8, 2008

As you know, we have been praying for Yanna for over a year. We have asked for God's blessings on her and our family and we have asked for God to open the doors wide so that we could bring her home. And you all have been praying with us all along. You have agreed with us that God brought Yanna into our lives and that He would one day restore her to our family. You have supported us and encouraged us and we are very grateful.

Thus, it is with great excitement that I tell you that we leave tomorrow, February 9th, for our first official visit to St. Petersburg. While we won't be bringing Yanna home this time, this first visit officially begins the adoption on the Russian side and so marks a very important step in the process. Thus, we ask that you continue to pray earnestly for God's favor. On Tuesday, we will appear before the Russian authorities and officially declare our desire to adopt Yanna. We will then be taken to see her and we will visit with her several times over the course of the week. We will have medical check ups and we will submit papers to the court, petitioning for a hearing where the adoption case will be heard. Following this trip, that court hearing will be the next and possibly the final step. So, you can see how important it is that God cover us during this next week.

Once again then, we ask for your support and prayers. Please remember us on Tuesday; pray for a great meeting with the authorities and for a great time with Yanna. Pray that we will meet only open and receptive hearts throughout the process. Pray for the logistics, for our transportation and for wisdom by those who are guiding and translating for us. And finally, pray for Yanna, for patience, strength, and assurance that she will not be anxious but will feel nothing but the unconditional love that God has given us for our children. Pray that this goes well and smoothly and that we are back in Russia soon for a final hearing. And in all things, give thanks for the blessing this journey has been.

One other note of interest, I have asked many times for God to act miraculously, to demonstrate that He is the one behind this by moving in a mighty way to bring Yanna home. While I have yet to see that one big miracle, God has given us many little ones. One such miracle is associated with this trip. As it turns out, we will be there during Yanna's birthday. We will arrive Sunday evening and will be able to spend Monday with Yanna; during that visit, we plan to celebrate her birthday! So, one year to the day after she left, we will be with her in St. Petersburg and will be there for her birthday.

Sometimes, you simply have to stand and marvel at the goodness of our God!

Thank you again for your prayers and support.

Blessings,

Allen

The process of arranging travel documents for a trip to Russia can be daunting. First, you need a visa to enter the country. But, to apply for a visa, you have to have been invited by some organization with official standing. Thankfully, all of our travel back and forth had prepared us for this and that was fortunate because the invitation had come barely three weeks before the actually appointment date was set. So, we had to move fast. We needed to arrange for someone to stay with our other children. I had to arrange coverage of my classes and other responsibilities at work. We also needed to pull together some money, lots of it, in the form of a sizeable stack of neat, new $100 bills. I'm not going to tell you exactly how much we carried because I'm not altogether sure that we didn't violate some rules by bringing that much currency into the country without declaring it. I will explain though that the money was denominated in new $100 bills because that is the form with which the Russians were the most comfortable and which they could most easily exchange for rubles. And this money was meant for Justin's office. Indeed, this is how he ran his operation and how he paid his various bills and staff. The money also represented a significant percentage of his overall fee. We were to take it and give it to Nina; Justin would then credit our account. There were no wire transfers, no bank charges and no paperwork to be completed in Russia. We simply handed Nina a large manila envelope full of money and that was that.

Well, that was how it was supposed to have worked at least. Unfortunately, though, I made two nearly serious errors in my completion of this otherwise simple task. First, I assumed that my bank would have a large supply of new $100s. So, I didn't go to get the money until two days before the trip. Apparently, few small town banks keep that many new $100s just lying around. So, it took a day, and considerable legwork by the people at our bank, just to pull it all together. Second, I assumed Justin would appreciate having some record of the payment to Nina. So, when I handed her the envelope, I also handed her a receipt that I had prepared and I that asked her to sign. She very nearly kicked me out of the car. What is more, by the time I reached our hotel room later that afternoon, Justin was calling my room, chastising me for the break in protocol and instructing that I should never again ask for another receipt or signature. Here again though, I'm getting ahead of myself; so, let me back up and tell you a bit about this trip.

We left from Atlanta and flew through Milan, Italy. There are no direct flights between Atlanta and St. Petersburg, and the many trips we had made had afforded us the opportunity to sample several of the various options for midway points along the way. Paris was easy in terms of scheduling but Charles de Gaulle airport was always a bit of an experience. Amsterdam was very nice and very easy;

Moscow, on the other hand, was neither nice nor easy. This time, though, we decided to try something new; we even planned to stay over in Milan for a day on the return trip. So, we flew out of Atlanta late one afternoon and arrived first in Milan and then in St. Petersburg in the late afternoon of the next day. In all it was about 12 hours of flight time but about 18 hours of travel, counting driving and layovers. With the eight-hour time difference, we ended up arriving about two – three hours, plus one day, after we had left.

We were met at the internal arrival terminal of the Pulkova, St. Petersburg, airport by three people Nina, Oksana and Alexi. Nina was Justin's registered agent in St. Petersburg. She was a short, stern woman, perhaps in her mid 60s, who had been a member of the communist party back in the days of the Soviet Union. Nina was direct, transactional and all business. She did laugh but mostly at her own jokes and she was much more interested in talking than she was in listening. Oksana was her translator and was taller and younger but no less stern and humorless. I will say that Oksana was the absolute best translator I had ever heard. She was certified by the Russian court as being able to translate legally binding documents, which means that a judge would sign documents translated by Oksana, even though the judge could not actually read those documents herself. Oksana could also translate orally in real time. In other words as Nina or the social worker or some other official spoke, Oksana could stand next to us and translate without any noticeable delay. And she could respond to those people by translating our English back into Russian, again without any noticeable delay. It was truly amazing to watch. So, Oksana went everywhere with us. Finally, was Alexi. Alexi drove the car, a brand new Range Rover, tricked out with heated leather seats, a top shelf sound system, and chrome wheels. He rarely spoke and, when he did, he spoke only to Nina or Oksana. He was a good driver though, able to create space where none was apparent, and to make progress on crowded streets (and sidewalks) when others were stuck in place. This was the car out of which Nina nearly tossed me, when I dared to ask for a receipt. Oh, well, lesson learned and we were off from the airport to the Hotel Moscow at the southern end of the downtown district of St. Petersburg.

The schedule included many of the things I described previously. We were treated very well, almost like celebrities, and accorded every courtesy almost everywhere we went. When we checked into our hotel, Oksana handled everything, including our registration, room assignment and internet access. When we went for our physical exams, the hospital had organized a special process for "the Americans." We were hosted in a nice lounge with about a dozen or so other parents, who were working with other adoption agencies. Once our blood had been drawn and tested, we were served cakes, coffee, tea, etc. and entertained by various physicians and staff who would stop by to make conversation. Every few minutes, a different person would come in to get a couple and take them, along with their translators, to various parts of the hospital for different diagnostic procedures. Over the course of the day, Cricket and I would be taken to have blood drawn, to get a chest x-ray, to take an EKG, etc. Each time, we would go together and Oksana would come along to translate. Of course, American standards of privacy and modesty are unheard of in Russia and, try as they might, the whole process was still very foreign to most of the visiting parents. We were paraded around in our underwear and examined by the Russian doctors while our translators stood by and translated. The whole process took four to five hours and killed one whole day. At the end of that day, we paid $1,500 per person, in cash, for the report that would be submitted to judge along with our dossier.

We also had a long visit with a social worker. This took place at Yanna's orphanage and included our friend Lydia, the orphanage director. The social worker talked to us about our home and family, about plans for Yanna and about the process by which we had come to know her. The interview also included Yanna, for a short time at least. We listened as the social worker asked Yanna about us, about her time with us and about the time since our first meeting. She even asked Yanna if she wanted to be adopted by us. Thankfully, Yanna responded, "yes." Here again, this process took several hours, including travel time and waits. That took care of another day.

We visited the office of a notary, who had us sign a number of documents which she then counter-signed and bound with fancy looking red thread. Most of these were process-related documents, certifying that we were who we said we were, that we had been given Yanna's family history and medical records, that we agreed to abide by the terms of the adoption court's orders, etc. We often didn't fully know everything we were signing. We simply did as Oksana directed, and then paid the bill at the end of the visit. Day after day, sometimes with Yanna, sometimes by ourselves, Oksana, Alexi and occasionally even Nina, would usher us through a maze of offices and officials. Sometimes, the purpose was clear; sometimes, it was not, but each stop brought us closer to the next step in the process and closer to the prize at the end of the journey.

There was one other event on this visit that is worthy of note. To explain, recall that we were there during Yanna's birthday. This was an unexpected blessing; after all, we had no input into or control over the date of our appointment and visit. Still, we were happy to be there for the occasion. Yanna was turning 11 and she wanted us to celebrate with her. In fact, we had planned to host a party for her at the orphanage. Her counselors would have celebrated her birthday anyway, but knowing that we were coming, they invited us to attend and we offered to bring the cake and ice cream. Well, that was the plan at least. When we explained our intentions to Oksana and Nina, they were not happy. Their attitude was, we were on a tight schedule, and there was no time for such foolishness as this. Moreover, they were paid to do a job that involved the adoption of a child.

They were not paid to escort us around in pursuit of our own priorities. We were rather surprised at this reaction and upset at the prospect that we might miss Yanna's party. We had promised we would be there; we had planned extra time in the schedule, and we wanted to see our daughter. So, not knowing what else to do, we called our friend Masha. Masha had been one of people I had met during my original visit to St. Petersburg. She had attended one of my talks at St. Petersburg Christian University and had helped us on several of our previous visits, taking over as our translator and guide when Sasha moved to the United States for graduate school.

Masha arranged a car that took us up to the orphanage where we would have Yanna's party. Masha stayed with us while we visited with Yanna, her friends and counselors. Masha even arranged with Lydia to allow us to take Yanna out of the orphanage for the night and back to our hotel on the other side of the city. Of course, we were excited by this, as was Yanna.

By the time the party ended and we started back for the hotel, the car we had hired was long departed. So, Masha decided we would return to the hotel via the Metro. Like many European cities, St. Petersburg has an excellent subway system, called the Metro. As an interesting bit of trivia, I have been told that the St. Petersburg Metro is the deepest, on average, of any subway system in the world. If you've ever been to St. Petersburg, you'll understand why. The city is built in a low area, around the Gulf of Finland; in fact, the city is spread over several islands and, much like Amsterdam or Miami, it is crossed with numerous rivers and canals. So the Metro had to be built deep in the bedrock, beneath the marshes and mud.

There was a Metro station in the basement of our hotel and there was a Metro station just a few blocks walk from Yanna's orphanage. So, it made sense that we would travel this way. Moreover, it was an adventure for us and for Yanna, and it gave us an opportunity to see more of our newest, favorite city. Given that, our group of four set out from the orphanage around 9:00 at night. It was a cold night in late February, but we were bundled up nicely. I had even worn the bright blue jacket that I often wore when our family went skiing. We walked the four or five blocks to the Metro station and descended the long escalator to the trains. To get to our hotel, we would need to take two different trains. First, we would ride to the center of town to the enormous and centrally located Nevsky Station. Once there, we would change to another line that would take us the rest of the way to our hotel.

Yanna was excited to be with us on her birthday and excited to be on the Metro, and, like most excited 11 year olds, was chattering away, talking to Masha and to us. Recall that, by this point, I was feeling very comfortable in Russia, and, so, I was talking back just as readily. So, the 20 or so minutes it took to arrive at the Nevsky Station passed quickly. Once there, we disembarked onto a platform to cross over to the next line and await our train. Apparently, it was during this time that we began to attract attention. As I mentioned, we were all talking away, loudly and mostly in English. I was also dressed in a bright blue ski parka, wearing a pair of Nike cross-trainers and an Atlanta Braves baseball cap. Looking back on it now, I suspect I stood out like a beacon.

The oddest part of the whole experience was how natural it felt, right up to the moment that it began to feel unnatural and then dangerous. We were all standing together on the platform, waiting on our train. The platform was crowded, but no more so than I have found in other cities at this hour of the night. As the train approached, people crowded to the edge a bit, but this too felt very normal. When the train in front of us stopped, people immediately began trying to both get off and through the crowd on the platform, just as the people on the platform were trying to push their way through and onto the train. I just tried to move along with the crowd, pushing my way against an immovable mass of bodies in front of me. As I said, it all felt very normal until I happened to look sideways, into the train car I was trying to board. I was shocked by what I saw; the train was virtually empty. This crowd around me was just that, a crowd around just me! All at once I put it together, I was being surrounded by a mob. That mob was trying to push me off the train and back onto the platform where, separated from my party, I would be mugged.

In my panic, I was able to reach forward and grab a vertical pole just inside the train car. I could now hear Masha yelling in Russian and Cricket yelling in English at the members of the mob still inside the train. I also became aware that I was being punched the ribs, just under my right arm. My guess is they were trying to break my grip on the pole. I was also aware of hands being jammed into my pants pockets, while other hands pulled and tugged at my jacket, presumably trying to tear it open. The entire ruckus lasted perhaps 30 seconds or so. Not long, but long enough to delay the closing of the train doors, which set off an alarm. With an alarm sounding, the mob released me and simply began to melt away.

I remember thinking to myself, as I got through the scrum and securely onto the train, "I wonder which of these people were among the actual muggers?" To find out, I turned quickly to look around and find the attackers; however all I saw was a group of young men who stared back into the car blankly and simply walked off casually, either off the train before the doors closed or off to another car as the train got underway. As I got my wits about me, it all made sense. I had been warned of these very types of situations and this one had unfolded just as I had been warned it might. It was a set up. The whole thing, the crowd on the platform, the people on the train, the traffic jam at the door, all of it was orchestrated for effect. The goal was to separate me from the party, to push me off the train and, presumably, to rob me once I was alone on the platform. Although I didn't lose anything other than a Nutrigrain bar I had been carrying in my breast pocket, it was frightening and I was shaken.

The most frightening thing, though, occurred to me afterward, as Masha, Cricket and I began discussing it. Suppose the scrum had escalated into a real fight and the police had come. Suppose those police had questioned us, Masha and even Yanna. Suppose they had found out that we had Yanna out of the orphanage before the adoption was complete. Although unlikely, this one event could have set in motion a series of events that would have resulted in our being disqualified completely from the adoption process. As I sat there and thought about it, I became more and more distraught and more and more apprehensive about the future. We simply could not take chances like this again. We had to do everything right, for the sake of the process.

Apparently, Yanna had performed a similar analysis and come to a similar conclusion. Indeed, the next day she went with us on a short walk outside of our hotel. We went into the Alexander Nevsky Monastery across the street from our hotel. There, she requested that we buy her a small wooden icon, depicting an angel. Once back at the hotel, Yanna gave the icon to me and explained that it was for my protection.

The rest of the visit was no less busy but was much less eventful. We took Yanna to have pictures made for her new passport and for her immigration visa. We went back to the original office of the committee on orphans, where we filed our medical reports as well as the reports from the social worker. We enjoyed spending the weekend at the hotel with Yanna, and we laughed out loud when she used the bidet as a foot-wash. We even had a little time for a lunch with Nina, Oksana and Alexi. Interestingly, Nina picked the restaurant and Nina did most of the talking while we were there. Alexi joined us, at Nina's invitation, and everyone ordered from the menu liberally, food, drinks, desserts, the whole shebang. Of course, once the bill came, Nina simply said to the waiter, "give it to the Americans." Sigh. I don't suppose I was surprised, nor were we unwilling to pay, but we did feel a little used.

At the conclusion of the week, Oksana and Alexi returned us to the airport for the trip home. Just before dropping us off at the curb, they gave us a thick package, which we were to return to Justin, once we were back in the States. They also gave us a series of instructions for our next trip. We had to have that album of pictures that I mentioned earlier. We were to include pictures of our home, of our other children, of our other children with Yanna, etc. We had to have certifications from our physician that our other children were all in good health. We needed a few other documents, based on Nina's review of our dossier. And, of course, all of this new material would have to be apostilled. Perhaps the oddest instruction though was this; we were to bring no less than ten bottles of perfume, from a very short list of brands that included Coco Channel, Clive Christian and Hermes. That's right, perfume, along with packages and wrappings sufficient for each bottle. No generics, no cheap stuff, don't wrap any of them ourselves, just bring them. We'll see you on your next visit.

The Beginning of the End: Act Two

In some ways, those final days before that final visit were a lot like the final days of that metaphorical pregnancy I mentioned in the beginning. We spent a lot of time just sitting around, waiting. We kept our cell phones charged and with us, so as not to miss Justin's call. We tried to never leave town, and we planned little or nothing that couldn't be quickly and easily changed. We also kept a stack of supplies that we would need to pack and carry with us at the ready on the floor of our bedroom. After 14 months of prayer and persistence, waiting and working, we were like a coiled spring, ready to snap into action the moment the restraint was released. And it was in early March when the time finally came. "Allen," Justin said, "the court has scheduled your hearing." I had waited for more than a year to hear those words; so, when they finally came, they came as no surprise and, in just a very few days, we were packing and preparing to go. Naturally, I wanted to send a note to all those following and praying on our behalf.

March 21, 2008

> *This past year has been difficult for Cricket and me, for our family, for Yanna, and even many of you. It's been difficult to love a child and to feel that she belonged to us and yet to know that she was beyond our reach. It's been hard to be good parents to a daughter 8 time zones away while still trying to be good parents to our other children here at home. It's been hard to avoid commitments, to leave our schedules open, and to*

pour time, energy and resources into an effort that at times seemed it would never end. It has been a difficult season, a time that we will never forget.

Yet, as trying and tiring as it has been, we would do it all again. The simple truth is that we love Yanna, just like any one of our other children and we could never abandon the effort to bring her home. So, it is with a heart full of joy that I tell you our court date is set and we leave for Russia this Easter Sunday. We will arrive on Monday, do paperwork on Tuesday and have our court hearing on Wednesday. If things go well, Yanna will be ours that evening. We do not know exactly when we will be able to bring her home. It could be as soon as the next week or it could take longer. But, Lord willing, at the end of that hearing, she will be Yanna Amason and we will all be very happy indeed.

I am also joyful about this process. While it has been hard, on all of us, it has taught me to appreciate the patience and love of our Heavenly Father. Just as we have pursued Yanna, so does He pursue us. Just as our hearts have ached with the separation, so does He grieve for us and desire to be with us. And just as we will celebrate when Yanna comes home, so is there rejoicing in heaven when one of us returns to the Lord. The reality of it is simply overwhelming. Just to be with us, Jesus gave up his very life. And as painful as that was, He would do it all again, just because He loves us. Amazing love indeed!

Well, I didn't mean to preach. I simply wanted to share with you our joy and to ask that you continue to pray. Wednesday will be an important day; please pray that every thing about it will be covered by God's presence and peace. Thank you for your support; we hope to have good news for you soon.

Blessings,

Allen

The court date was to be March 26, 2008, a Wednesday. We got word of the court date about three weeks prior to our projected arrival date of Sunday, March 23, and we immediately purchased our airline tickets and began the paperwork to obtain our visas. We would travel through Moscow's Sheremetyevo airport this time. We would have to go to Moscow after the adoption anyway, so that Yanna could be issued an American immigrant visa and cleared by the U.S. Embassy. So, flying in through Moscow in both directions made the arrangements cleaner. The plan was for our oldest son, Chase to stay away at college, doing what he was supposed to do there until he heard from us. He was also to remain on call, so to speak, should he be needed in some way to assist with his younger siblings. The younger kids would finish school on Friday, March 21, after which we would take them to my mother's house, about an hour and a half north of us. They would remain there until we returned, even though that meant missing a significant amount of school. We would fly out of Atlanta on Saturday, March 22, arriving in St. Petersburg on Sunday, March 23. We would spend all day Monday with Nina, Oksana, Lydia and the social worker, prepping our materials and preparing ourselves, mentally, for what was to come. We had been advised in advance that this trip would be all business. There would be no birthday parties, no family reunions and no disruptions of the schedule for unofficial purposes. Everything followed a script that had been developed by the court. Our job was to play the role assigned to us flawlessly and without deviation. And, this time, we were determined to do just that.

Part of that role was the preparation and you will recall we were to bring perfume and lots of it. Now, I had no real sense of how this perfume would be used, where we would get it or what it cost. I just assigned that whole job to Cricket, assuming it would be easily and quickly handled. As I learned though, it was not quite that easy. The brands Nina had requested, in the sizes required, easily ran to more than $1,000. That alone was frustrating, after we had spent so much already. But the transporting of this contraband was also problematic. When carried together, ten large bottles of perfume make for a heavy load; they also take up an awful lot of room. Moreover, because the bottles are glass, they are subject to breaking. If they were to break, it would ruin everything in the suitcase along with the perfume itself. What is more, it would leave us without all the things Nina had asked us to bring. So, the perfume was becoming something of a stumbling block as we prepared to leave.

I'll remind you now, as I was reminded then, of the many scriptures that caution us about anxiety. Over and again it is made clear that God cares for us, that He is involved and active, even in the intimate and small details of our lives. Like a loving father, He cares about things that concern us, despite the fact that those things to Him must seem terribly trivial. He knows the plans He has for us; He is the one who announces the end from the beginning. And, so, He does not worry and neither should we. Nevertheless, worry is one of the things we do and do well. And we were worried about this perfume, not so much because of the costs or the logistics of transporting it. Rather, we were worried because of what the perfume represented. This was something we had been given to do and so it was something that we needed to get right, so that everything else would go smoothly. Well, as if to remind us yet again that He was in charge of this entire process, God used this perfume and our anxiety over it to demonstrate His faithfulness with two powerful miracles.

The first of these miracles came in the form of a woman from our church. She had heard about this rather unusual challenge we had been given, and she offered to help. As it turned out, she was the manager of the cosmetic area of a local department store. The store was part of a large national chain and so dealt directly with the firms that made the types of perfume we needed. She asked Cricket what we needed and then asked the various manufacturers' sales representatives for help. They provided her with all new bottles of samples and extras, sufficient to provide us with everything we needed. What a shock and a blessing that was.

Now, all we had to do was get it over there. Again though, we were worried, worried about the prospect of entrusting this stuff to the belly of the various aircrafts on which we would fly and worried about the bottles breaking while in the gentle graces of the baggage handlers in Atlanta, Moscow and St. Petersburg. So, we decided to pack it in our carry-on. I should tell you that we are, normally, luggage-checkers. Because of my work, we tend to fly a good bit and are blessed to usually get our luggage checked for free. So, we normally just pack what we need, check it in at the counter and not worry about keeping up with suitcases as we move around the airport and the plane. So, we're no experts when it comes to packing carry-on luggage. Still, we knew that we could take a small, roll aboard with us in the cabin of the plane. And we knew we would need to carry a number of small but important things with us. So, we packed our large cases, which would be checked in, and then we also packed one other small case to carry on. In that small case was the money we would need, a single dress outfit for each of us to wear to the court hearing, the photo album we had assembled to present to the judge, the adoption dossier for the family that would follow us, and the ten large bottles of expensive perfume, each wrapped in tissue and carefully tucked throughout the case.

By now, it has occurred to many of you already that this carry on bag, carefully packed as it was, was also in complete violation of FAA regulations. Indeed, it has been just a few short years prior to this trip that the FAA issued regulations limiting the ability to take liquids and gels in carry on luggage. No bottle could be larger than three ounces and all had to be packed in a clear plastic bag, no larger than one quart. So, not only had we broken one rule, we had broken every rule relating to transporting of liquids. We had ten fancy bottles, each wrapped individually in paper, stuck throughout the case, in and around our clothes, so as to cushion them from any impact. You can imagine then the scene at the TSA station in Atlanta, when this case went through the scanner. The line stopped; the agents pulled the case aside and asked to whom it belonged. They then took us aside, opened the case and began inspecting its contents, while asking us a variety of questions. At once, it occurred to both of us what we had done and our panic began to mount.

Cricket started crying and trying to explain the situation to the TSA agent. I began racing through various alternatives in my mind. Perhaps, I could take the bag back to the counter and check it in there. Perhaps, I could retrieve our previously checked luggage and move the perfume into it. As I was busy thinking, busy stumbling for explanations and busy blaming myself for making this dumb mistake and as Cricket was busy asking tearfully for forgiveness and understanding, the TSA agent looked at me and winked. He then winked again and again in a slow, pronounced fashion. He then looked at us both and said, "I'm sorry, I must have something in my eye and just can't see you all very clearly." And then he winked again. It took a moment; I guess we're not the quickest on the uptake when it comes to this sort of thing. But we soon deciphered his intention; he was going to let us pass, with the case and the perfume! And he was using this exaggerated wink and explanation about something in his eye to signal us. Upon realizing this, Cricket thanked him profusely; I thought she was going to hug him and blow the whole deal. But he simply winked again and told us we were free to go. We hurriedly closed the case and took it away, toward our gate. Yes, the God who created heaven and earth, the God who parted the Red Sea and who raised Jesus from the dead is sovereign and reigns over all of creation, even over the TSA.

The flight and arrival were much like the many trips we had made previously. We arrived at Pulkovo Airport, Terminal 2, and were met by Oksana and Alexi. They took us to the Hotel Moscow, near the city center of St. Petersburg. They got us checked in; we were even in the same room as we had been on the previous trip. They collected the various documents that Nina had requested and they made arrangements to pick us up the next morning. We were giddy with excitement. But that excitement would fade.

On the Sunday before we left on this trip to Russia, our Sunday School class at church gathered around us, to lay hands on us and pray. They had been intimately involved with our journey throughout and they wanted to make sure we were covered and protected. So, they prayed for us, for Yanna, for our other children, for our travel and for all the arrangements that would make the trip effective. Following the prayer and as we were leaving the class, a good friend pulled us aside. "God has given me a word of encouragement, and warning, for you," he said. He told us that, in his vision, we were successful in adopting Yanna. However, the process would be hard. "Something will happen," he said. He couldn't say what that something was; he had simply sensed that something would happen to disrupt the proceeding. Some roadblock or hurdle would arise and stand in the way. When it did, we were simply to pray all the more and then trust God to remove it, and He would.

Honestly, I rather blew this off and I'm sure hurt the feelings of my friend. We had covered every base and planned for every contingency. The adoption agency was the best, and we had followed their instructions precisely. We were loved and favored by the orphanage director and by the social worker. We had demonstrated commitment to Yanna through our many trips to see her, and we could prove with our dossier and photo album that she would be welcomed, loved and cared for in our home. So, what could wrong?

The first hint of trouble came during our meeting with Nina and the Lydia on Monday. Nina explained that she had consulted with the court clerk and was expecting a long and difficult hearing. She also explained to us the process. We would be called into a courtroom that was closed to all but the participants. Those participants included the judge, the clerk, the child advocate, who was called the "prosecutor," Lydia, the social worker, Cricket and me, and Oksana, our translator. Oksana though was present only to translate and was, otherwise, to be completely invisible. There would be a large table, in front of the judge's bench, where Lydia, the social worker and the clerk would sit. The prosecutor would sit at another table, in front of us. We sat on a wooden bench, facing the judge, with Oksana in a chair behind us. When called upon, we were to rise and speak, answering the judge's questions in minimal fashion, while standing still, with our hands at our sides. We were not to volunteer information, not to speak to one another during the proceeding, and not to cross our legs or "slouch" while sitting and watching the process unfold. This all seemed strange but, to me at least, underscored the methodical and detailed approach of Justin and his staff. Nothing was left to chance. So, on the morning of hearing, I was excited to meet Oksana and Alexi in the lobby of the hotel, excited to drive across town and to walk into the courthouse, and excited to enter the courtroom and to find everything exactly has Nina had described it.

Oksana led us to the bench where we sat down. At the center of the room was a large partition, with the judge's desk behind it. Behind the desk were two normal-sized windows, with old, drab curtains. Between the windows was a large seal, with the double-headed eagle symbol of the Russian Federation. Between where we sat and the desk and slightly to the left was a small desk where a stern looking woman, in a military-styled uniform was seated. This was the prosecutor. To the right, but also between our bench and the judge, was a large table with perhaps six chairs. Lydia, the social worker and one or two other officials were seated at the table. One of those officials was the woman from the committee office. We had met her on our last visit. The whole set up was very familiar and might well have been any courthouse in the U.S. And, just like in the U.S. we all rose to our feet when the judge entered. She walked through a door on the wall to our right. She walked in front of us, between the table and the prosecutor, as she made her way across the room, to a position up and behind her desk. After some words in Russian, directed at the entire room, everyone, including us, sat down. And with that, the hearing was underway.

The judge was a short woman; you might even call her stumpy; short but thickly built, with broad shoulders, very little neck, and a head that seemed disproportionately large. She had short, thick gray hair that was cut just below the ears but that framed her face symmetrically. She did not smile much. In fact, I don't recall her smiling at all, ever. Rather, she came across as angry or perhaps just irritated. It was that look we all have when absolutely nothing has gone right and now we have one more unpleasant task to accomplish. Starting from the moment she walked in, we could sense the level of anxiety in the room begin to rise. It was, perhaps, 10:30 on Wednesday morning when the hearing actually started. We had brought some snacks, which we had eaten in the waiting area prior to the hearing. So, we were comfortable and rested, ready to do battle, if necessary, for our daughter.

The first few minutes involved the judge reading our official adoption request. She then asked some questions of

Lydia, of the prosecutor and of the social worker. All seemed to be pro forma and going according to plan. Then, the judge asked me to stand, which I did, respectfully. As she peered at me, her frustration seemed to grow. She held in her hand my passport, which we had submitted upon our arrival. She flipped through it, in a dismissive, almost abusive fashion; clearly she knew its contents and had already decided what she was going to say. "I see you have been to Russia many times" she sneered. "Were you paid to come here?"

In my entire life, I can remember skipping school only once. Oh, sure, I cut the occasional class or ducked out early for some made up reason. I also left sometimes for legitimate purposes but under the guise of some other purpose. Such as a family vacation, my parents would want to get an early start and so would pick me up early, telling the staff in the office that I had some sort of appointment. But that was all minor stuff, penny ante. Actually skipping school meant lying to your parents, letting them think you had gone to school but, then, intentionally going somewhere else, and staying there more or less for the whole day. I did that only once; it was my sophomore year in high school and our entire school of some 2,000 students was being forced to make up a snow day, during our spring break. We, a pronoun that in this case included my brother, our circle of friends and me, all agreed it was ridiculous, and we weren't going to do it. Call it standing up to the man, perhaps, but we all decided to skip school and go to the beach. I grew up in a resort area, and the beach was close by. So, my brother, our best friend and a host of others from our high school skipped school for the day and went to the beach instead.

The flaw in our otherwise ingenious plan was that this was our hometown. So, many of the people we encountered that day at the beach knew us and knew our parents and families. Given that, it should have come as no surprise when my mother greeted me the next morning, by asking, "how was your day yesterday?" Her smile and pleasant tone belied her intentions. She knew she had something on me and she knew that I wasn't quite sure just how much she actually knew. So, for me, the dilemma was simple. I could assume she knew everything. In which case, I would come clean completely, perhaps incriminating myself and my friends. Alternatively, I could assume she new very little, in which case I would deny everything, thereby running the risk of being caught in a lie and making my judgment more severe. Finally, I could assume she knew something but not everything, in which case the strategy was to play dumb and make her work for every little bit of information. In so doing, I would also buy time and with that time I could better discern exactly what she knew and how best to deal with her anger over it. I remember thinking through these various options, as my mother asked me, accusingly, about that previous day.

Well, the entire situation was now replaying itself in a courtroom in St. Petersburg. And, again, I was faced with a dilemma. This judge knew she had something on me. This time, however, the problem was, I wasn't quite sure what I had done wrong. No, we were not supposed to have taken Yanna out of the orphanage. In fact, Nina and the social worker had told us the day before that we were not to volunteer or ever admit to that. I could manage that. We would simply say that we had visited Yanna in the orphanage, which we had. We could admit to seeing her outside of the orphanage, but only under the supervision of Russian citizens, who had been authorized by Lydia, the orphanage director, to take her out. And all of that was true, even if only partially so. Otherwise though, we had not done anything. So, I felt the truth was on my side. Still, the look from this judge was menacing and telling. She clearly thought there was something nefarious here, something she could uncover with aggressive, clever and, if possible, intimidating questioning.

And so she began; she accused me of using Yanna as a means to come to Russia for the sake of earning a profit through business. She accused me of breaking Russian law by taking Yanna out of the orphanage before I had legal standing in the Russian system. She accused me of being a part of an elaborate conspiracy, which rewarded orphanage workers with trips and gifts if they would identify and present Americans like us with adoptable children. It was a very, very tough interrogation and, throughout, I had to stand, virtually at attention, answering every question with respect and deference. It was hard, very hard. I listened politely as she spit out her questions, why had I come to

Russia so quickly? Why had I picked Yanna, rather than some other child? Why would I want a fourth child, when I already had three? Why was I now a member of a Methodist church, when my marriage certificate noted that I had been married in a Presbyterian church? She would cut me off in mid explanation, loudly proclaim her disbelief at my answers and openly accuse me of lying. It was humiliating and frustrating.

You see, what I wanted to do was to put her in her place. Oh, yes, she was clever in her questioning, baiting me and then pouncing on whatever answer I provided. But she wasn't nearly as good as she thought. I would have loved to explain how her system had failed Yanna and so many others. I would have loved to have turned the issue on her and accused her of failing to even ask the right questions. I would have loved to joust with her and to win this rhetorical fight she had picked. But I had not come to Russia to win an argument. Since that day at the sunglasses case, I had been on a quest to redeem my daughter. In much the same way Jesus had come to redeem us, I had to focus on the bigger picture and on the ultimate goal. What humiliation did Christ endure for us? What suffering and frustration did the apostles and the saints endure through the ages, to provide an example for us? These were the thoughts that flooded my mind as I stood there, taking her abuse, without giving into it. During this long period of questioning, the prosecutor also joined in, asking me to explain things about Yanna that a father would be expected to know. What was her favorite color? What was her favorite subject in school? What did she want to be when she grew up? How could I know these things without getting to know her? Yet, it was because I invested so much in getting to know her that I was now being accused of usurping the process and bypassing Russian law.

When my time in the dock was finished, the judge told me to sit; she then repeated the process with Cricket. It had lasted fully 90 minutes with me and almost as long with Cricket. Again, the questions were much same, in content and tone. Why had Cricket come to Russia so often? Who had given her the authority to visit Taganrog, where the children had gone to camp? Was she a Christian and, if so, was she secretly coming to Russia in an effort to convert people away from their Orthodox faith? Who was this Sasha that we kept referencing and what standing did she have to meet and interact with Yanna? Again, it was hard to sit through and hard to watch. I spent the whole time, perhaps 75 minutes or so, praying for my wife. I asked God to strengthen her legs and back, as standing at virtual attention for that amount of time was challenging. I asked that God would quicken her mind, so that she would not be caught in the snares that this judge was setting before her. I asked that she would have control of her emotions and not break down, not get angry and show neither weakness nor defiance in the face of these accusations. I prayed for her because I love her but also because it gave me a way occupy my mind. Otherwise, I would have exploded with anger over this unjust and inappropriate treatment.

Somewhere in this process, they invited Yanna into the courtroom. I remember marveling at how these aggressive, almost mean-spirited women softened when they questioned Yanna. They were sweet and maternal in their demeanor and their line of questions. Was Yanna happy in the orphanage? Did she like school? How had she met us and how had she enjoyed her time with us? Did she want to be in our family and move to America? She was so brave, and I was so proud of her. She simply answered each question, honestly and respectfully. She considered us her real parents, and she wanted to live with us. She loved her new house, her new siblings and her new pets. She believed Cricket would be a good mother and that I would be a good father. She wasn't quite sure what I did for a living but she believed I worked hard and that I was good at what I did. So, she didn't fear for her future with us. It really was very sweet. But it lasted only ten minutes or so, and then Yanna was excused from the courtroom and taken back to the orphanage.

Meanwhile this judge turned her attention to the social worker and to Lydia. The argument between Lydia and the judge was spectacular. The judge accused Lydia of profiting through the marketing of the children in her care. Lydia responded that she was a decorated director, with more than 30 years of service in the care of orphaned children, and she knew best how to care for them. The heated, almost hostile exchange continued until the judge threatened to hold Lydia in contempt and to turn her over to the authorities for potential indictment. At that, and only at that, did Lydia back down and show deference. The poor social worker fared even worse. While Lydia was older, experienced and mature, the social worker was young and unfamiliar. The judge accused her of cutting corners, of favoring us in the hopes of profiting from us, and of not working sufficiently hard to find all of Yanna's relatives and to notify them of the pending adoption. Again, we just sat and watched, bewildered and praying for God to intervene and stop this assault.

Of course, even through all of this (and it lasted several hours), we tried to keep our eyes on the prize. We had come to adopt our daughter and if this dreadful and long hearing was the toll that we had to pay in order to cross that bridge, then we would simply have to pay it; however, the whole thing took a surprising and fearful turn at about 3:30 in the afternoon. The judge had just finished her questioning of the social worker. She was clearly angry, tired and frustrated that she had failed in her attempt to derail us. So, in her frustration, she announced that she was suspending the hearing. She simply did not want to hear any more from us or to discuss this adoption any further. She did want to see one other document; it was a form, signed by Yanna's biological grandmother, acknowledging that she understood that Yanna was being adopted by an American family. It didn't matter that this biological grandmother had no parental rights or standing in this matter. It didn't matter that this biological grandmother had never visited Yanna during the time she was in the orphanage. It didn't matter that the social worker had tried to get this form signed before the hearing but had been unable to do so because she was never able to find this biological grandmother at the last address in the records. The judge wanted this form by the next day. She also wanted some time to consider what she had heard thus far. It was a stunning turn of events. We had come into that courtroom fully well believing we would walk out with our daughter. As it was though, we left with nothing but anxiety and uncertainty. That night, I wrote the following letter to all those who were now following our journey.

March 26, 2008

> *Today was a long day and a disappointing one. I had hoped to be writing with happy news. Unfortunately, Yanna is still not ours. The judge was very upset that we had visited Yanna before the official adoption process began. She was also upset about a number of other things that dealt more with procedures and paperwork. And so, she suspended the hearing, after about 3 hours and scheduled a reconvening tomorrow at 12:00 (5:00 a.m. EDT). She will issue her ruling then. Of course, these issues are not the real problem. Instead, we believe our battle is a spiritual one and not against flesh and blood. And it was obvious that a spirit of darkness was in control of that hearing.*

> *We truly believe God brought Yanna to us and that we were supposed to love her as if she was our own. We also believe that God brought us here to Russia, so that we could bring Yanna home. So, today's experience was really a surprise and we were quite shaken. For now, we simply wait for*

tomorrow. The hearing will continue then and the judge simply wants to see some additional documents, that have almost nothing to do with us. If these documents are in order, then she will give us a decision.

So much about this is hard to understand. For now though, we have no choice but to persevere. Scripture says that the righteous will live by faith; but that can be hard. Yanna is our daughter and we have tried to be good parents to her, from a distance. All we want is to fullfill that relationship and bring her home. Unfortunately though, we are powerless in this battle. So, we have to rely entirely on our Heavenly Father. Thus, we ask you to pray.

Tomorrow will be a big day and tonight will be a long night. So, please pray against fear and dispair. Pray also that the documents will be in order and that the judge and the authorities will look upon us favorably. Finally, please pray that God's will be done in this matter. The desire of our heart is to bring Yanna home and to do so next week. More than even that though, we want to know God's will and to follow it. So, please pray that He will reveal Himself tomorrow and show us clearly what He would have us do.

Thank you for your prayers and your support.

Blessings,

Allen

It was indeed a very long night. I remember spending a part of it in the Alexander Nevsky Monastery; the same one we had visited previously. The monastery was founded in

1710 and sits on a sprawling complex of buildings and gardens, wedged tightly between two busy streets and a river. It contains some of the oldest structures in St. Petersburg, as well as a cemetery where several greats of Russia culture and history are buried. The famous composer Pyotr Tchaikovsky is buried there, as was the novelist, Fyodor Dostoyevsky. It really was a neat and peaceful place. At its center was a modest chapel. Not nearly so imposing as St. Issac's or as grand the Church of the Spilt Blood, this chapel somehow felt more natural, intimate and genuine. You entered by walking underneath the entrance arch and then down a long exposed walkway, where dozens of St. Petersburg's poor and infirm sit and beg for donations. We had taken Yanna into this chapel, and she had generously given money and encouragement to each and every person along the way. This time, though, we were the ones who needed encouraging. So, we went into the chapel and sat down to pray.

The next morning came and we awoke in the hotel. After a light breakfast, we met Oksana and Alexi and headed to the courthouse. We were scheduled for 9:00 but, upon arriving, found only Nina there. The judge had not yet arrived and neither Lydia nor the social worker, were there either. Nina explained that Lydia had gone with the social worker to assist in finding the biological grandmother and in securing her signature. The judge had approved this, along with the subsequent delay, sending word to her clerk, who told Nina, who then told us. So, we sat and waited. There was no waiting room, so to speak. Instead, there was a hallway. It was the hallway just outside the courtroom door. It had two small couches, a couple of straight-backed wooden chairs, a men's room, a ladies' room, and several other doors. Most of these doors never opened. We spent hours in that hallway, listening mostly to either Nina or Oksana, as they spoke on the phone. Other than that, there simply wasn't much to do. Yanna was not there this time; there was no reading material, at least none in English. And neither Nina nor Oksana was particularly chatty. So, we sat and waited.

While I was far from confident, I was at least content. We had prayed hard that God grant us the desire of our hearts. We wanted Yanna as our daughter, in every sense of the word. But we were also comfortable that we had fought the good fight. We had loved this child with no conditions. We had worked and sacrificed for her. We had faithfully pursued our daughter through what was now 15 months of effort and stress. We had broken some rules, yes, but we had done so for the right reasons. Moreover, there were many, many important rules that we had not broken. Indeed, we had taken no short cuts in this. We had done everything we had been asked to do, following the letter of the process affirmatively and strictly. Our only transgressions came in the form of going beyond the rules, loving and parenting Yanna before the adoption was official. And, if that was a crime, then we would have to stand comfortably in our guilt. And so, we had prayed that it was now all in God's hands; we had done what we were supposed to have done. We could leave the outcome in the hands of almighty God.

I believe it was around 12:30 when Lydia and the social worker arrived. They had the document with the signature of the biological grandmother and they were both very casual and happy. Nina, meanwhile, was as relaxed as could be, chatting away on one call or another as if she were in her own office. The court clerk would occasionally walk down the hallway, discussing matters of this and that with Nina. I remember thinking about how close and casual they looked together, as if there were no stress in this at all. I reflected on my most recent conversation with Justin; I had spoken to him the evening before, just before we left the hotel to go to the chapel in the monastery. "Allen," he said, with his thick and gravely accent, "this judge, she's crazy. But don't worry about her; she will give you the kid tomorrow. She has no choice in the matter." What did he mean she has no choice? It crossed my mind that this whole thing was more show than substance.

Regardless, within just a few minutes of the two ladies' arrival, the courtroom doors opened, and Oksana announced that it was time for us to enter. As before, the prosecutor was seated at the table to our left. We were back on the bench, with Oksana behind us. Lydia and the social worker were seated at the large table to our right. After just a couple of moments, we were all asked to stand, the judge came in and sat down at her desk. We all sat down and we were under way. The judge asked to see the document, which the social worker presented. There was some short conversation between the two of them, something about how the permanent address of the biological grandmother was some sort of collective home, with just one phone and mailbox. The judge then asked if we had anything else to add, to which we responded, "no." So, she stood up and announced that she would be back shortly with her decision.

I don't believe she was out of the room for more than a minute. In fact, it was almost comical; the door closed behind her and, then, seemingly, reopened almost immediately. We all stood, out of respect, as she walked across the floor, up the steps to her chair and then was seated behind her desk. With almost no expression and with no eye contact with us, she read a prepared order, that she had carried with her from her office. The order was mostly legal-ease, recounting the specifics of our filed request, of Yanna's position in the orphanage system and in the database. But, after two or three pages of that, she finally got to the crux of the matter. What happened next was the subject of my next newsletter.

March 27, 2008

Since early last January, I have wondered how this day would feel. I have imagined it, thought about it, tried to anticipate how I would react when the judge finally announced the decision. As it turns out, it was different and more overwhelming than I had expected.

With virtually no expression, the judge read "it is my decision that the petition be granted and that the petitioners be registered as the official parents of the child..." And with that, Yanna Zubova became Yanna Amason, and we had our fourth child. It was all I could to stand still; Cricket broke down and cried. At once, the journey was over and we were Yanna's official parents. We will be several more days in Russia, processing the paperwork necessary to bring Yanna home and to provide her with immediate U.S. citizenship. The best estimate puts us back next Thursday. But as of today, Yanna is ours!

There are no words to express our gratitude for all your prayers and support. I had hoped to have an eloquent message for you, some deep theological meaning that I could convey from all of this. But the truth is, I am completely poured out emotionally. All I can offer right now is gratitude. To all of you who have prayed for Yanna for so long, to all of you who have supported us throughout this process, to everyone who has covered for us and helped us with the logistics of this past year, we say thank you. More than that though, we thank God for his mercy and faithfulness. Ours is a great God - greater than I can express. All I have needed, he has provided; great is his faithfulness indeed!!

Blessings,

Allen

The End of the End

Recall there is a final step in this five-step adoption process that I have not yet described and that we had not yet taken. It was now Thursday afternoon, March 27, 2008 and Yanna was ours; the judge had just signed an order saying so; however, just because she was our daughter in the eyes of the Russian government did not mean she was ours in any practical sense. We still could not travel with her freely nor could we bring her home to the United States. I don't really know what I had been thinking about this; I suppose I hadn't been thinking about it at all. But it does make sense that it would take time to secure things like a passport and an immigration visa. But think for a moment about what has to happen to get those types of documents. You typically need things like identification, birth certificates, pictures, notarized application documents, proof of citizenship, et cetera. More importantly in this instance though, you need to have all of that in your own name; however, Yanna's name had just been changed. So, this fifth step involved changing all of Yanna's domestic identification documents into her new name. It also involved changing all of the parental names on her identification documents from those of her biological parents to ours. Then, it involved taking all of these new documents and using them to apply for her entrance documents to the U.S. As an old Jewish friend was fond of saying when he faced daunting tasks or exasperating circumstances, "oy."

Thankfully, though, there was a plan for all of this. Indeed, as it turns out, my favorite Romanian adoption agent had thought of everything. And he, Nina and Oksana had orchestrated this particular part of the score to perfection. As I mentioned, it was Thursday afternoon. If, we could get the appropriate government office to issue a new birth certificate, in Yanna's new name, and to do it that afternoon, then we could take that birth certificate and use it to secure all of the other documents on Friday.

Step one, though, was to get the judge to waive the "ten-day" rule. This rule was a bit strange. It ordered that every adoption, though fully in force at the moment of the judge's order, required ten days to become effective. As it was explained to us, the purpose was to allow parents the option to back out. In essence, the judge would rule in favor of the adoption; the parents would then travel back home and have a week or so to consider the gravity of their actions. When they returned, in ten business days, they could go directly to the orphanage and collect their child; however, if they simply never came back, then the adoption was off. I suppose there could be some logic in that in the case of a newborn child and first time parents. But it made no sense whatsoever in our situation. We had been pursuing this adoption relentlessly for 15 months; ten more days would do nothing but leave us more frustrated and leave Yanna more distressed. While everyone readily acknowledged this, it made no difference in the eyes of the law. This was a rule and it could only be waived for a specific set of reasons.

Understanding this, I was given a script to read before the judge, at the very end of our hearing. When the judge asked for final comments, I was to stand and read this statement, explaining how a widespread case of flu was raging through the orphanages in St. Petersburg, and then explain how that flu posed a special risk to Yanna. If she were to catch the flu, it would delay her exit from Russia and so delay the start of her schooling in the U.S. And so, because of this risk, we requested that the customary ten-day waiting period be waived, in this one instance. Nevermind that there had been only one case of flu in Yanna's orphanage and nevermind that Yanna was going to be homeschooled for the remainder of that academic year. Reading the script was necessary to give the judge a reason to waive the order. And she did just that. Again, with virtually no expression and without so much as a glance towards us, she said that she agreed with our petition and she signed an order, waiving the ten-day waiting period. With that, we could immediately collect Yanna and begin the process of changing and securing the necessary documents.

I won't bore you with all the details of traveling from office to office and from waiting room to waiting room, as necessary to get each new piece of information. I will tell you, though, that it was all part of a well-choreographed dance that Justin and Nina had planned out very well. For example, remember all that perfume? Well, we now saw it used for its intended purpose. Before we would enter an office, Nina would take one of the bottles and one of the gift bags we had brought. She would write a little note, pack the bottle with paper in the bag, and then enter the office. Upon entering, she would walk past the lines of people, directly to a particular clerk. She would often just set the bags on the clerk's desk or on the floor beside the desk. She would talk with the clerk a bit and then either give him or her a package of documents or pick up a package of documents. Then, she would turn and leave, leaving the gift bag where she had placed it. She would walk passed all the people waiting in line and tell us that we were ready to go. This same sequence was repeated in nearly a dozen different offices, all across St. Petersburg until, at the end of the day, sometime in the middle of the afternoon on Friday, Nina declared that we were finished and so were ready to go pick up Yanna.

Part of our agreement with the orphanage was that we would host a party for Yanna and her group, before taking her away. And, so, we did; we brought cakes, candies and drinks, and we enjoyed our visit with the staff and children of the orphanage. It was strange really; we knew we were there to take Yanna away, and we knew that, once we left, we likely would never be back. Still, it was nice to spend this last time with them, to thank them for all they had done for Yanna, to collect all of Yanna's school work, records, pictures, clothes and other belongings and allow her time to tell her friends goodbye. As I said, it was strange and bittersweet. We were exuberant over the judge's decision and the conclusion of our long journey. But, for Yanna, as well as for all the other children in the orphanage, this had to be a difficult moment.

I remember one little boy telling Yanna that she was lucky, and then asking her knew if she knew why we had picked her. That one comment has stuck with me all these years. Why did we pick her? Gosh, I don't know; it was just because in that one instant as I sat and reviewed the database, her picture appealed to me in a way that no other picture did.

It was because in that one instant at the sunglass counter, I knew that she was my daughter in exactly the same way my biological children were. And, so, she was different from every other child at that orphanage and everywhere else in the world. Why her and not someone else? That's an incisive and complicated question that is impossible to answer, absent an understanding of God's will and grace. But, even with that understanding, I can't tell you exactly why. I can only see how I was a small part of a larger process and how that process paralleled God's plans for our lives. He pursues us; He pours energy and effort into us. He drops us breadcrumbs designed to lead us home. And, ultimately, He gave up his deity and His earthly life, just so that we could be with Him. Why us? Well, because He loved us. To those who can understand that, no other explanation is necessary; to those who cannot, no other explanation is possible.

The bittersweet tension reached its climax as we walked out that familiar set of double doors. All of Yanna's belongings were packed into a suitcase, which we loaded into Alexi's car. The six of us, Alexi, Nina, Oksana, Cricket, Yanna and I, then loaded into the car. Cricket and I were flooded with emotion, but Yanna was even more so. Because the car was crowded and because of her overwhelming feelings, she simply crawled into Cricket's lap and, as the car drove out of the gate of the orphanage, fell sound asleep.

Rather than return to the Hotel Moscow, we went to the apartment of our friends Mike and Olga. They were in the U.S. at the time and had offered it to us for as long as we needed it. We would be in St. Petersburg throughout the weekend, leaving for Moscow on Sunday and would appreciate having a comfortable and economical place to stay. So, Alexi dropped us off at the front door, where we introduced ourselves to the doorman, picked up a key to the upper floor apartment, went up stairs and settled in. It was the same feeling we had with our previous three children, when we brought them home from the hospital after their births. This was our first night at home with our new daughter, and we were happy and ready for some rest.

From here, things would move pretty quickly. We would stay in St. Petersburg as tourists all day Saturday and Sunday. We would see the sights, buy some souvenirs, and get anything any of the three of us needed before we left for Moscow. To understand why we had to go to Moscow, think of getting out of Russia as the opposite of getting in. To adopt Yanna, we had to get the approval of the U.S. government first, then we had to get the approval of the Russian government. To leave with our new daughter though, we first had to get the approval of the Russian government. Once we had obtained that, which we now had done, we then had to gain the approval of the U.S. government. To do that, we would have to go to the U.S. Embassy in Moscow. We would travel on the overnight train from St. Petersburg to Moscow, a distance of about 450 miles; the trip would take about eight hours.

Helping us arrange all of this was Masha. Of course we knew Masha well and liked spending time with her. She was an excellent tour guide, a real student of Russian history and culture and a darn good translator. Also, as I had learned during that harrowing event in the St. Petersburg Metro, she could be scrappy and tough. All in all, I was glad to have her around.

We did our sightseeing in St. Petersburg, visiting the Hermitage and St. Issac's Cathedral. We also bought some oil paintings at an arts festival at a park by the river. Those paintings were framed and still hang in our house. They are a great reminder of our unbreakable connection to Russia as well as of the trip on which we brought Yanna home. We ate at some classic Russian restaurants as well as the occasional McDonald's. In the two days we had, we saw quite a lot. Remember, we had never had the opportunity to be tourists on any of our previous trips. So, we made the most of the time we had.

When Sunday evening rolled around, Masha arranged for a car to take us to the train station. We had booked two first-class sleeping births side by side. Each would accommodate two people; Masha and Yanna in were in one while Cricket and I were in the other. It was late when we pulled out of the station. We all four stood together at the window until St. Petersburg passed into the darkness. We then went to our respective rooms and went to sleep. I don't know whether it was the gentle rocking of the train, the darkness of the rural Russian night, or the knowledge that I was leaving St. Petersburg this time with my daughter, but I remember sleeping very well.

We awoke the next morning as the train was pulling into the Moscow station. I remember thinking that this was the same station through which Yanna had traveled on her way to America that first time. So, it seemed a friendly place, and I was happy, if a bit overwhelmed, to be there. While we were still gathering our luggage and preparing to exit the train, we were greeted by another of Justin's employees. Sadly, I can't remember this woman's name. But she was likely in her 50's, with dark hair and a slight build. She also had a very soft appearance, certainly unlike many of the Russian women we had encountered in the court system and at the government offices. She seemed almost compassionate toward us, which was very different from what we were used to with Nina and Oksana. So, we liked her straight away. She also spoke English, which meant that we did not need a translator. Like Nina and Oksana, though, she was all business and highly efficient.

Because we had arrived early, she had arranged for us to go through the process as soon as we arrived. With good fortune and good timing, we would complete everything we needed to complete that day. So, we met our driver and went straight from the train station to the American Embassy. There, Yanna was given a medical exam, her immunization records were authenticated and certified, we stood in some lines, completed some forms and, then, submitted a bundle of documents to the embassy staff. We were then given a time at which we were to return in the afternoon. Upon our return, we waited a short time again before we were brought to a small counter, where a State Department employee, a woman of perhaps no more than 30, asked us a few questions and then, in perfect Russian, spoke with Yanna for about ten minutes. After that, we were told we could go. We were also told that our package of materials, which included all of Yanna's immigration materials, along with her passport and visa, would be ready for pick up on Wednesday. Until then, we were on our own.

We had booked our flight home for Thursday. Flights bound for Atlanta, and other parts of the eastern U.S. tended to leave Moscow in the morning, around 11:00. So, it would be unwise to try do any adoption related work on the day of the departure. It was better to get everything completed and then leave the next day. That is what we did. Once we had picked up the material from the Embassy on Wednesday, we would spend one more night and then leave for the airport Thursday morning. Masha would go with us, see us onto the plane and then take the next flight back to St. Petersburg. It was a good plan if everything came together as expected. But it also left us with the better part of two full days to kill in Moscow, which we managed to do very well.

I remember a lot about those next two days in Moscow. I remember touring the Kremlin. Recall Masha was a student of Russian history and culture; she gave us a wonderful tour, which included viewing the corpse of Ivan the Terrible. I remember our hotel, or rather, our hostel.

Because we had arrived on such short notice and because we needed to be near the Embassy, we didn't have many good options for lodging. The hotels in Moscow were all either sold out or prohibitively expensive. So, Masha arranged for us to get a private apartment, inside a hostel, which she often used when she brought tours into the capital. It was not a five-star accommodation, but it was safe and comfortable and the location, along Stary Arbat (or Old Arbat) Street, less than a mile from Red Square was hard to beat. I remember eating at the Hard Rock Café and the Starlight Diner, as well as from the carts of various street vendors along Red Square. Yanna would actually eat the hotdogs that these vendors were grilling; Cricket and I stuck with the ice cream and the bottled juices. I remember the credit card system being shut down for a day because of some security threat back in the U.S. The result of that minor catastrophe was that I had to get cash from the ATM, cash sufficient to sustain us in one of the world's most expensive cities for two days.

I remember riding the subway out to a large hill near Moscow State University. From the top of this hill, I could see much of the city, along with the old Olympic Village, from the 1980 summer Olympics. Two ruffian boys who walked near us called to Yanna, asking her to come spend some time with them. I just held her hand all the more tightly. I remember strolling along a street one afternoon and overhearing Yanna refer to Cricket and me as "the Americans" as she asked a question of Masha. It was both amusing and telling, as it underscored her challenge in learning to accept and trust us as her real parents. I remember spending hours in the Starbucks on Stare Arbat Street. It had high-speed wifi, which would allow me to connect my computer and Skype back home. I remember in one of those calls arranging with Chase and with my assistant, to reserve a limousine, which would bring our other three children to the airport in Atlanta and then pick us up and take us all, the whole six of our family, back home to Athens. On our last night in Moscow, I remember eating dinner at a Mexican restaurant; I believe it was the only Mexican restaurant in all of Moscow. All in all, it was a great and a productive visit to a great city. But what I remember most about that visit was how badly I wanted to get home.

The opportunity finally came on Thursday, April 3. We woke early, packed and made our way downstairs. There was a our driver and Justin's agent, ready to load us up and send us on our way. The agent gave us a final bundle of documents, along with some instructions on how to answer questions at the passport control desk at the Sheremetyevo airport. We then climbed into the car and were soon making our way through the security line. Masha would fly out of the domestic terminal, Sheremetyevo 1, while we would fly out the international terminal, Sheremetyevo 2. But she stood by us, right up to the point where we had to present our passports and tickets. Then, she waived us goodbye. There was short conversation with the passport control agent, who needed proof that we were now Yanna's adoptive parents and were able to take her with us out of the country. But we did as we had been instructed, and the passport control agent was soon satisfied. At that point, we entered the gate area, and I began to feel the pressure lift.

Like a diver trapped beneath the water, I had been swimming desperately for the surface, longing for that fresh air that was just beyond the barrier. As we walked toward the gate, it was like seeing the rays of sunlight through the water, and, as the plane lifted off the ground, it was as if I had suddenly and finally broken through. After more than a year of agonizing effort, we had finally made it and were on our way home.

We were in a 767, wide-body jet. I was able to get the three middle seats; so Cricket and I both had aisle seats, while Yanna sat in between the two of us. We talked for bit, ate lunch when it was served and enjoyed explaining to Yanna how to use the in-flight entertainment system. We had been in the air for several hours when we came to the realization that Yanna was not going to sleep a wink during the entire 12-hour flight. Cricket and I, on the other hand, were both completely exhausted. And, at some point, just an hour or two after we finished lunch, Cricket was fast asleep. And it was then that I took out my computer for the final installment of my newsletter.

April 3, 2008

"Do not be afraid, for I am with you; I will bring your children from the east..." (Is. 43:)

Since we began working to adopt Yanna, this verse has been our sanctuary, the strong tower to which we ran when we were troubled and the light to which we looked in moments of darkness. It is a promise centuries old. Yet, we claimed it as our own and held to it steadfastly, believing that we had followed God's leading throughout.

And now we are on a plane somewhere over the Atlantic Ocean, with Yanna sitting between us, returning home to our other children who will be waiting at the airport. If ever there was a time that I was humbled by God's goodness and faithfulness, it is now.

I'm still not sure why this took so long or just what I was supposed to learn from it. One thing that God has taught me though is the awesome responsibility of being a father. I don't mean that in the usual sense. Rather, I have come to understand that as a father, I stand for a season in the role of God. I have the opportunity to show my children true, unconditional love. I have the chance to cultivate in them a spirit of openness, to prepare them to receive and to trust fully in the love of their heavenly father. How hard it must be for a child to accept the love of God if they never had a loving father of their own.

What I have come to realize is that, for the past 15 months, my job has been to love Yanna and to pursue her, with no conditions. I had to love her first; I had to pour in the energy and the effort. And in so doing, I was modeling for her the love of her heavenly father. What an honor, what awesome charge! To be a father to the fatherless and in so doing to point her to her true, eternal father, I can think of nothing more important.

And so, I thank you one last time. Your intercession was felt and appreciated throughout. Moreover, even though this will be my final letter to you, I want to ask for your continued prayer and support. Integrating Yanna into our family will be a challenge for us all. Each day there will be new things to learn and new issues to resolve. Still, the same God who made that promise so long ago remains active today; he neither slumbers nor sleeps and what he starts he finishes. So, please continue to remember us in your prayers as you have these past months and we will continue to walk forward, trusting in God's goodness and faithfulness.

Blessings,

Allen

www.ingramcontent.com/pod-product-compliance
Lightning Source LLC
LaVergne TN
LVHW051229080426
835513LV00016B/1486

* 9 7 8 0 6 9 2 5 2 8 8 2 2 *